Napoleon Bonaparte

by John S. C. Abbott

Napoleon, finding his proffers of peace rejected by England with contumely and scorn, and declined by Austria, now prepared, with his wonted energy, to repel the assaults of the allies. As he sat in his cabinet at the Tuileries, the thunders of their unrelenting onset came rolling in upon his ear from all the frontiers of France. The hostile fleets of England swept the channel, utterly annihilating the commerce of the Republic, landing regiments of armed emigrants upon her coast, furnishing money and munitions of war to rouse the partisans of the Bourbons to civil conflict, and throwing balls and shells into every unprotected town. On the northern frontier, Marshal Kray, came thundering down, through the black Forest, to the banks of the Rhine, with a mighty host of 150,000 men, like locust legions, to pour into all the northern provinces of France. Artillery of the heaviest calibre and a magnificent array of cavalry accompanied this apparently invincible army. In Italy, Melas, another Austrian marshal, with 140,000 men, aided by the whole force of the British navy, was rushing upon the eastern and southern borders of the Republic. The French troops, disheartened by defeat, had fled before their foes over the Alps, or were eating their horses and their boots in the cities where they were besieged. From almost every promontory on the coast of the Republic, washed by the Channel, or the Mediterranean, the eye could discern English frigates, black and threatening, holding all France in a state of blockade.

One always finds a certain pleasure in doing that which he can do well. Napoleon was fully conscious of his military genius. He had, in behalf of bleeding humanity, implored peace in vain. He now, with alacrity and with joy, roused himself to inflict blows that should be felt upon his multitudinous enemies. With such tremendous energy did he do this, that he received from his antagonists the most complimentary sobriquet of the one hundred thousand men . Wherever Napoleon made his appearance in the field, his presence alone was considered equivalent to that force.

The following proclamation rang like a trumpet charge over the hills and valleys of France. "Frenchmen! You have been anxious for peace. Your government has desired it with still greater ardor. Its first efforts, its most constant wishes, have been for its attainment. The English ministry has exposed the secret of its iniquitous policy. It wishes to dismember France, to destroy its commerce, and either to erase it from the map of Europe, or to degrade it to a secondary power. England is willing to embroil all the nations of the Continent in hostility with each other, that she may enrich herself with their spoils, and gain possession of the trade of the world. For the attainment of this object she scatters her gold, becomes prodigal of her promises, and multiplies her intrigues."

At this call all the martial spirit of France rushed to arms. Napoleon, supremely devoted to the welfare of the State, seemed to forget even his own glory in the intensity of his desire to make France victorious over her foes. With the most magnanimous superiority to all feelings of jealousy, he raised an army of 150,000 men, the very elite of the troops of France, the veterans of a hundred battles, and placed them in the hands of Moreau, the only man in France who could be called his rival. Napoleon also presented to Moreau the plan of a campaign in accordance with his own energy, boldness, and genius. Its accomplishment would have added surpassing brilliance to the reputation of Moreau. But the cautious general was afraid to adopt it, and presented another, perhaps as safe, but one which would produce no dazzling impression upon the imaginations of men. "Your plan," said one, a friend of Moreau, to the First Consul, "is grander, more decisive, even more sure. But it is not adapted to the slow and cautious genius of the man who is to execute it. You have your method of making war, which is superior to all others. Moreau has his own, inferior certainly, but still excellent. Leave him to himself. If you impose your ideas upon him, you will wound his self-love, and disconcert him."

Napoleon, profoundly versed in the knowledge of the human heart, promptly replied. "You are right, Moreau is not capable of grasping the plan which I have conceived. Let him follow his own course. The plan which he does not understand and dare not execute, I myself will carry out, on another part of the theatre of war. What he fears to attempt on the Rhine, I will accomplish on the Alps. The day may come when he will regret the glory which he yields to me."

These were proud and prophetic words. Moreau, was moderately victorious upon the Rhine, driving back the invaders. The sun of Napoleon soon rose, over the field of Marengo, in a blaze of effulgence, which paled Moreau's twinkling star into utter obscurity. But we know not where, upon the page of history, to find an act of more lofty generosity than this surrender of the noblest army of the Republic to one, who considered himself, and who was deemed by others, a rival--and thus to throw open to him the theatre of war where apparently the richest laurels were to be won. And he know where to look for a deed more proudly expressive of self-confidence. "I will give Moreau," said he by this act, "one hundred and fifty thousand of the most brave and disciplined soldiers of France, the victors of a hundred battles. I myself will take sixty thousand men, new recruits and the fragments of regiments which remain, and with them I will march to encounter an equally powerful enemy on a more difficult field of warfare."

Marshal Melas had spread his vast host of one hundred and forty thousand Austrians through all the strongholds of Italy, and was pressing, with tremendous energy and self-confidence upon the frontiers of France. Napoleon, instead of marching with his inexperienced troops, two-thirds of whom had never seen a shot fired in earnest, to meet the heads of the triumphant columns of Melas, resolved to climb the rugged and apparently inaccessible fastnesses of the Alps, and, descending from the clouds over path-less precipices, to fall with the sweep of the avalanche, upon their rear. It was necessary to assemble this army at some favorable point;--to gather in vast magazines its munitions of war. It was necessary that this should be done in secret, lest the Austrians, climbing to the summits of the Alps, and defending the gorges through which the troops of Napoleon would be compelled to wind their difficult and tortuous way, might render the passage utterly impossible. English and Austrian spies were prompt to communicate to the hostile powers every movement of the First Consul. Napoleon fixed upon Dijon and its vicinity as the rendezvous of his troops. He, however, adroitly and completely deceived his foes by ostentatiously announcing the very plan he intended to carry into operation.

Of course, the allies thought that this was a foolish attempt to draw their attention from the real point of attack. The more they ridiculed the imaginary army at Dijon, the more loudly did Napoleon reiterate his commands for battalions and magazines to be collected there. The spies who visited Dijon, reported that but a few regiments were assembled in that place, and that the announcement was clearly a very weak pretense to deceive. The print shops of London and Vienna were filled with caricatures of the army of the First Consul of Dijon. The English especially made themselves very merry with Napolcon's grand army to scale the Alps. It was believed that the energies the Republic were utterly exhausted in raising the force which was given to Moreau. One of the caricatures represented the army as consisting of a boy, dressed in his father's clothes, shouldering a musket, which he could with difficulty lift, and eating a piece of gingerbread, and an old man with one arm and a wooden leg. The artillery consisted of a rusty blunderbuss. This derision was just what Napoleon desired. Though dwelling in the shadow of that mysterious melancholy, which ever enveloped his spirit, he must have enjoyed in the deep recesses of his soul, the majestic movements of his plans.

On the eastern frontiers of France there surge up, from luxuriant meadows and vine-clad fields and hill sides, the majestic ranges of the Alps, piercing the clouds and soaring with glittering pinnacles, into the region of perpetual ice and snow. Vast spurs of the mountains extend on each side, opening gloomy gorges and frightful detiles, through which foaming torrents rush impetuously, walled in by almost precipitous cliffs, whose summits, crowned with melancholy firs, are inaccessible to the foot of man. The principal pass over this enormous ridge was that of the Great St. Bernard. The traveler, accompanied by a guide, and mounted on a mule, slowly and painfully ascended a steep and rugged path, now crossing a narrow bridge, spanning a fathomless abyss, again creeping along the edge of a precipice, where the eagle soared and screamed over the fir tops in the abyss below, and where a perpendicular wall rose to giddy heights in the clouds above. The path at times was so narrow, that it seemed that the mountain goat could with difficulty find a foothold for its slender hoof. A false step, or a slip upon the icy rocks would precipitate the traveler, a mangled corpse, a thousand feet upon the fragments of granite in the gulf beneath. As higher and higher he climbed these wild and rugged and cloud-enveloped paths, borne by the unerring instinct of the faithful mule, his steps were often arrested by the roar of the avalanche and he gazed appalled upon its resistless rush, as rocks, and trees, and earth, and snow, and ice, swept by him with awful and resistless desolation, far down into the dimly discerned torrents which rushed beneath his feet. At God's bidding the avalanche fell. No precaution could save the traveler who was in its path. He was instantly borne to destruction, and buried where no voice but the archangel's trump could ever reach his ear. Terrific storms of wind and snow often swept through those bleak altitudes, blinding and smothering the traveler. Hundreds of bodies, like pillars of ice, embalmed in snow, are now sepulchred in those drifts, there to sleep till the fires of the last conflagration shall have consumed their winding sheet. Having toiled two days through such scenes of desolation and peril, the adventurous traveler stands upon the summit of the pass, eight thousand feet above the level of the sea, two thousand feet higher than the crest of Mount Washington, our own mountain monarch. This summit, over which the path winds, consists of a small level plain, surrounded by mountains of snow of still higher elevation.

The scene here presented is inexpressibly gloomy and appailing. Nature in these wild regions assumes her most severe and sombre aspect. As one emerges from the precipitous and craggy ascent, upon this Valley of Desolation, as it is emphatically called, the Convent of St. Bernard presents itself to the view. This cheerless abode, the highest spot of inhabited ground in Europe, has been tenanted, for more than a thousand years, by a succession of joyless and self-denying monks, who, in that frigid retreat of granite and ice, endeavor to serve their Maker, by rescuing bewildered travelers from the destruction with which they are ever threatened to be overwhelmed by the storms, which battle against them. In the middle of this ice-bound valley, lies a lake, clear, dark, and cold, whose depths, even in mid-summer, reflect the eternal glaciers which soar sublimely around. The descent to the plains of Italy is even more precipitous and dangerous than the ascent from the green pastures of France. No vegetation adorns these dismal and storm-swept cliffs of granite and of ice. Even the pinion of the eagle fails in its rarified air, and the chamois ventures not to climb its steep and slippery crags. No human beings are ever to be seen on these bleak summits, except the few shivering travelers, who tarry for an hour to receive the hospitality of the convent, and the hooded monks, wrapped in thick and coarse garments, which their staves and their dogs, groping through the storms of sleet and snow. Even the wood which burns with frugal faintness on the hearths, is borne, in painful burdens, up the mountain sides, upon the shoulders of the monks.

Such was the barrier which Napoleon intended to surmount, that he might fall upon the rear of the Austrians, who were battering down the walls of Genoa, where Massena was besieged, and who were thundering, flushed with victory, at the very gates of Nice. Over this wild mountain pass, where the mule could with difficulty tread, and where no wheel had ever rolled, or by any possibility could roll, Napoleon contemplated transporting an army of sixty thousand men, with ponderous artillery and tons of cannon balls, and baggage, and all the bulky munitions of war. England and Austria laughed the idea to scorn. The achievement of such an enterprise was apparently impossible. Napoleon, however was as skillful in the arrangement of the minutest details, as in the conception of the grandest combinations. Though he resolved to take the mass of his army, forty thousand strong, across the pass of the Great St. Bernard, yet to distract the attention of the Austrians, he arranged also to send small divisions across the passes of Saint Gothard, Little St. Bernard, and Mount Cenis. He would thus accumulate suddenly, and to the utter amazement of the enemy, a body of sixty-five thousand men upon the plain of Italy. This force, descending, like an apparition from the clouds, in the rear of the Austrian army, headed by Napoleon, and cutting off all communication with Austria, might indeed strike a panic into the hearts of the assailants of France.

The troops were collected in various places in the vicinity of Dijon, ready at a moment's warning to assemble at the point of rendezvous, and with a rush to enter the defile. Immense magazines of wheat, biscuit, and oats had been noiselessly collected in different places. Large sums of specie had been forwarded, to hire the services of every peasant, with his mule, who inhabited the valleys among the mountains. Mechanic shops, as by magic, suddenly rose along the path, well supplied with skillful artisans, to repair all damages, to dismount the artillery, to divide the gun-carriages and the baggage-wagons into fragments, that they might be transported, on the backs of men and mules, over the steep and rugged way. For the ammunition a vast number of small boxes were prepared, which could easily be packed upon the mules. A second company of mechanics, with camp forges, had been provided to cross the mountain with the first division, and rear their shops upon the plain on the other side, to mend the broken harness, to reconstruct the carriages, and remount the pieces. On each side of the mountain a hospital was established and supplied with every comfort for the sick and the wounded. The foresight of Napoleon extended even to sending, at the very last moment, to the convent upon the summit, an immense quantity of bread, cheese, and wine. Each soldier, to his surprise, was to find, as he arrived at the summit, exhausted with Herculean toil, a generous slice of bread and cheese with a refreshing cup of wine, presented to him by the monks. All these minute details Napoleon arranged, while at the same time he was doing the work of a dozen energetic men, in reorganizing the whole structure of society in France. If toil pays for greatness, Napoleon purchased the renown which he attained. And yet his body and his mind were so constituted that this sleepless activity was to him a pleasure.

The appointed hour at last arrived. On the 7th of May, 1800, Napoleon entered his carriage at the Tuileries, saying, "Good-by, my dear Josephine! I must go to Italy. I shall not forget you, and I will not be absent long." At a word, the whole majestic array was in motion. Like a meteor he swept over France. He arrived at the foot of the mountains. The troops and all the paraphernalia of war were on the spot at the designated hour. Napoleon immediately appointed a very careful inspection. Every foot soldier and every horseman passed before his scrutinizing eye. If a shoe was ragged, or a jacket torn, or a musket injured, the defect was immediately repaired. His glowing words inspired the troops with the ardor which was burning in his own bosom. The genius of the First Consul was infused into the mighty host. Each man exerted himself to the utmost. The eye of their chief was every where, and his cheering voice roused the army to almost super-human exertions. Two skillful engineers had been sent to explore the path, and to do what could be done in the removal of obstructions. They returned with an appalling recitasl of the apparently insurmountable difficulties of the way. "Is it possible ," inquired Napoleon, "to cross the pass?" "Perhaps," was the hesitating reply, "it is within the limits of possibility ." "Forward, then," was the energetic response. Each man was required to carry, besides his arms, food for several days and a large quantity of cartridges. As the sinuosities of the precipitous path could only be trod in single file, the heavy wheels were taken from the carriages, and each, slung upon a pole, was borne by two men. The task for the foot soldiers was far less than for the horsemen. The latter clambered up on foot, dragging their horses after them. The descent was very dangerous. The dragoon, in the steep and narrow path, was compelled to walk before his horse. At the least stumble he was exposed to being plunged headlong into the abysses yawning before him. In this way many horses and several riders perished. To transport the heavy cannon and howitzers pine logs were split in the centre, the parts hollowed out, and the guns sunks into grooves. A long string of mules, in single file, were attached to the ponderous machines of war, to drag them up the slippery ascent. The mules soon began to fail, and then the men, with hearty good-will, brought their own shoulders into the harness--a hundred men to a single gun. Napoleon offered the peasants two hundred dollars for the transporation of a twelve-pounder over the pass. The love of gain was not strong enough to lure them to such tremendous exertions. But Napoleon's fascination over the hearts of his soldiers was a more powerful impulse. With shouts of encouragement they toiled at the cables, successive bands of a hundred men relieving each other every half hour. High on those craggy steeps, gleaming through the midst, the glittering bands of armed men, like phantoms appeared. The eagle wheeled and screamed beneath their feet. The mountain goat, affrighted by the unwonted spectacle, bounded away, and paused in bold relief upon the cliff to gaze upon the martial array which so suddenly had peopled the solitude.

When they approached any spot of very especial difficulty the trumpets sounded the charge, which re-echoed, with sublime reverberations, from pinnacle to pinnacle of rock and ice. Animated by these bugle notes the soldiers strained every nerve as if rushing upon the foe. Napoleon offered to these bands the same reward which he had promised to the peasants. But to a man, they refused the gold. They had imbibed the spirit of their chief, his enthusiasm, and his proud superiority to all mercenary motives. "We are not toiling for money," said they, "but for your approval, and to share your glory."

Napoleon with his wonderful tact had introduced a slight change into the artillery service, which was productive of immense moral results. The gun carriages had heretofore been driven by mere wagoners, who, being considered not as soldiers, but as servants, and sharing not in the glory of victory, were uninfluenced by any sentiment of honor. At the first approach of danger, they were ready to cut their traces and gallop from the field, leaving their cannon in the hands of the enemy. Napoleon said, "The cannoneer who brings his piece into action, performs as valuable a service as the cannoneer who works it. He runs the same danger, and requires the same moral stimulus, which is the sense of honor." He therefore converted the artillery drivers into soldiers, and clothed them in the uniform of their respective regiments. They constituted twelve thousand horsemen who were animated with as much pride in carrying their pieces into action, and in bringing them off with rapidity and safety, as the gunners felt in loading, directing, and discharging them. It was now the great glory of these men to take care of their guns. They loved, tenderly, the merciless monsters. They lavished caresses and terms of endearment upon the glittering, polished, death-dealing brass. The heart of man is a strange enigma. Even when most degraded it needs something to love. These blood-stained soldiers, brutalized by vice, amidst all the honors of battle, lovingly fondled the murderous machines of war, responding to the appeal "call me pet names, dearest." The unrelenting gun was the stern cannoneer's lady love. He kissed it with unwashed, mustached lip. In rude and rough devotion he was ready to die rather than abandon the only object of his idolatrous homage. Consistently he baptized the life-devouring monster with blood. Affectionately he named it Mary, Emma, Lizzie. In crossing he Alps, dark night came on as some cannoneers were floundering through drifts of snow, toiling at their gun. They would not leave the gun alone in the cold storm to seek for themselves a dry bivouac; but, like brothers guarding a sister, they threw themselves, for the night, upon the bleak and frozen snow, by its side. It was the genius of Napoleon which thus penetrated these mysterious depths of the human soul, and called to his aid those mighty energies. "It is nothing but imagination," said one once to Napoleon. "Nothing but imagination!" he rejoined. "Imagination rules the world."

When they arrived at the summit each soldier found, to his surprise and joy, the abundant comforts which Napoleon's kind care had provided. One would have anticipated there a scene of terrible confusion. To feed an army of forty thousand hungry men is not a light undertaking. Yet every thing was so carefully arranged, and the influence of Napoleon so boundless, that not a soldier left the ranks. Each man received his slice of bread and cheese, and quaffed his cup of wine, and passed on. It was a point of honor for no one to stop. Whatever obstructions were in the way were to be at all hazards surmounted, that the long file, extending nearly twenty miles, might not be thrown into confusion. The descent was more perilous than the ascent. But fortune seemed to smile. The sky was clear, the weather delightful, and in four days the whole army was reassembled on the plains of Italy.

Napoleon had sent Bertlier forward to receive the division, and to superintend all necessary repairs, while he himself remained to press forward the mighty host. He was the last man to cross the mountains. Seated upon a mule, with a young peasant for his guide, slowly and thoughtfully he ascended those silent solitudes. He was dressed in the gray great coat which he always wore. Art pictured him bounding up the cliff, proudly mounted on a prancing charger. But truth presents him in an attitude more simple and more sublime. Even the young peasant who acted as his guide was entirely unconscious of the distinguished rank of the plain traveler whose steps he was conducting. Much of the way Napoleon was silent, abstracted in thoughts. And yet he found time for human sympathy. He drew from his young and artless guide the secrets of his heart. The young peasant was sincere and virtuous. He loved a fair maid among the mountains. She loved him. It was his heart's great desire to have her for his own. He was poor and had neither house nor land to support a family. Napoleon struggling with all his energies against combined England and Austria, and with all the cares of an army, on the march to meet one hundred and twenty thousand foes, crowding his mind, with pensive sympathy won the confidence of his companion and elicited this artless recital of love and desire. As Napoleon dismissed his guide, with an ample reward, he drew from his pocket a pencil and upon a loose piece of paper wrote a few lines, which he requested the young man to give, on his return, to the Administrator of the Army, upon the other side. When the guide returned, and presented the note, he found, to his unbounded surprise and delight, that he had conducted Napoleon over the mountains; and that Napoleon had given him a field and a house. He was thus enabled to be married, and to realize all the dreams of his modest ambition. Generous impulses must have been instinctive in a heart, which in an hour so fraught with mighty events, could turn from the toils of empire and of war, to find refreshment in sympathizing with a peasant's love. This young man but recently died, having passed his quiet life in the enjoyment of the field and the cottage which had been given him by the ruler of the world.

The army now pressed forward, with great alacrity, along the banks of the Aosta. They were threading a beautiful valley, rich in verdure and blooming beneath the sun of early spring. Cottages, vineyards, and orchards, in full bloom, embellished their path, while upon each side of them rose, in majestic swell, the fir-clad sides of the mountains. The Austrians pressing against the frontiers of France, had no conception of the storm which had so suddenly gathered, and which was, with resistless sweep, approaching their rear. The French soldiers, elated with the Herculean achievement they had accomplished, and full of confidence in their leader, pressed gayly on. But the valley before them began to grow more and more narrow. The mountains, on either side, rose more precipitous and craggy. The Aosta, crowded into a narrow channel, rushed foaming over the rocks, leaving barely room for a road along the side of the mountain. Suddenly the march of the whole army was arrested by a fort, built upon an inaccessible rock, which rose pyramidally from the bed of the stream. Bristling cannon, skillfully arranged on well-constructed bastions, swept the pass, and rendered further advance apparently impossible. Rapidly the tidings of this unexpected obstruction spread from the van to the rear. Napoleon immediately hastened to the front ranks. Climbing the mountain opposite the fort, by a goat path, he threw himself down upon the ground, when a few bushes concealed his person from the shot of the enemy, and with his telescope long and carefully examined the fort and the surrounding crags. He perceived one elevated spot, far above the fort, where a cannon might by possibility be drawn. From that position its shot could be plunged upon the unprotected bastions below. Upon the face of the opposite cliff, far beyond the reach of cannon-balls, he discerned a narrow shelf in the rock by which he thought it possible that a man could pass. The march was immediately commenced, in single file, along this giddy ridge. .... And even the horses, insured to the terrors of the Great St. Bernard, were led by their riders upon the narrow path, which a horse's hoof had never trod before, and probably will never tread again. The Austrians, in the fort, had the mortification of seeing thirty-five thousand soldiers, with numerous horses, defile along this airy line, as if adhering to the side of the rock. But neither bullet nor ball could harm them.

Napoleon ascended this mountain ridge, and upon its summit, quite exhausted with days and nights of sleeplessness and toil, laid himself down, in the shadow of the rock, and fell asleep. The long line filed carefully and silently by, each soldier hushing his comrade, that the repose of their beloved chieftain might not be disturbed. It was an interesting spectacle, to witness the tender affection, beaming from the countenances of these bronzed and war-worn veterans, as every foot trod softly, and each eye, in passing, was riveted upon the slender form, and upon the pale and wasted cheek of the sleeping Napoleon.

The artillery could by no possibility be thus transported; and an army without artillery is a soldier without weapons. The Austrian commander wrote to Melas, that he had seen an army of thirty-five thousand men and four thousand horse creeping by the fort, along the face of Mount Albaredo. He assured the commander-in-chief, however, that not one single piece of artillery had passed or could pass beneath the guns of his fortress. When he was writing this letter, already had one half of the cannon and ammunition of the army been conveyed by the fort, and were safely and rapidly proceeding on their way down the valley. In the darkness of the night trusty men, with great caution and silence, strewed hay and straw upon the road. The wheels of the lumbering carriages were carefully bound with cloths and wisps of straw, and, with axles well oiled, were drawn by the hands of these picked men, beneath the very walls of the fortress, and within half pistol-shot of its guns. In two nights the artillery and the baggage-trains were thus passed along, and in a few days the fort itself was compelled to surrender.

Melas, the Austrian commander, now awoke in consternation to a sense of his peril. Napoleon--the dreaded Napoleon--had, as by a miracle, crossed the Alps. He had cut off all his supplies, and was shutting the Austrians up from any possibility of retreat. Bewildered by the magnitude of his peril, he no longer thought of forcing his march upon Paris. The invasion of France was abandoned. His whole energies were directed to opening for himself a passage back to Austria. The most cruel perplexities agitated him. From the very pinnacle of victory, he was in danger of descending to the deepest abyss of defeat. It was also with Napoleon an hour of intense solicitude. He had but sixty thousand men, two-thirds of whom were new soldiers, who had never seen a shot fired in earnest, with whom he was to arrest the march of a desperate army of one hundred and twenty thousand veterans, abundantly provided with all the most efficient machinery of war. There were many paths by which Melas might escape, at leagues' distance from each other. It was necessary for Napoleon to divide his little band that he might guard them all. He was liable at any moment to have a division of his army attacked by an overwhelming force, and cut to pieces before it could receive any reinforcements. He ate not, he slept not, he rested not. Day and night, and night and day, he was on horseback, pale, pensive, apparently in feeble health, and interesting every beholder with his grave and melancholy beauty. His scouts were out in every direction. He studied all the possible movements and combinations of his foes. Rapidly he overran Lombardy, and entered Milan in triumph. Melas anxiously concentrated his forces, to break through the net with which he was entangled. He did every thing in his power to deceive Napoleon, by various feints, that the point of his contemplated attack might not be known. Napoleon, in the following clarion tones, appealed to the enthusiasm of his troops:

"Soldiers! when we began our march, one department of France was in the hands of the enemy. Consternation pervaded the south of the Republic. You advanced. Already the French territory is delivered. Joy and hope in our country have succeeded to consternation and fear. The enemy, terror-struck, seeks only to regain his frontiers. You have taken his hospitals, his magazines, his reserve parks. The first act of the campaign is finished. Millions of men address you in strains of praise. But shall we allow our audacious enemies to violate with impunity the territory of the Republic? Will you permit the army to escape which has carried terror into your families? You will not. March, then, to meet him. Tear from his brows the laurels he has won. Teach the world that a malediction attends those who violate the territory of the Great People. The result of our efforts will be unclouded glory, and a durable peace!"

The very day Napoleon left Paris, Desaix arrived in France from Egypt. Frank, sincere, upright, and punctiliously honorable, he was one of the few whom Napoleon truly loved. Desaix regarded Napoleon as infinitely his superior, and looked up to him with a species of adoration; he loved him with a fervor of feeling which amounted almost to a passion. Napoleon, touched, by the affection of a heart so noble, requited it with the most confiding friendship. Desaix, upon his arrival in Paris, found letters for him there from the First Consul. As he read the confidential lines, he was struck with the melancholy air with which they were pervaded. "Alas!" said he, "Napoleon has gained every thing, and yet he is unhappy. I must hasten to meet him." Without delay he crossed the Alps, and arrived at the head-quarters of Napoleon but a few days before the battle of Marengo. They passed the whole night together, talking over the events of Egypt and the prospects of France. Napoleon felt greatly strengthened by the arrival of his noble friend, and immediately assigned to him the command of a division of the army. "Desaix," said he, "is my sheet anchor."

"You have had a long interview with Desaix," said Bourrienne to Napoleon the next morning. "Yes!" he replied; "but I had my reasons. As soon as I return to Paris I shall make him Minister of War. He shall always be my lieutenant. I would make him a prince if I could. He is of the heroic mould of antiquity!"

Napoleon was fully aware that a decisive battle would soon take place. Melas was rapidly, from all points, concentrating his army. The following laconic and characteristic order was issued by the First Consul to Lannes and Murat: "Gather your forces at the river Stradella. On the 8th or 9th at the latest, you will have on your hands fifteen or eighteen thousand Austrians. Meet them, and cut them to pieces. It will be so many enemies less upon our hands on the day of the decisive battle we are to expect with the entire army of Melas." The prediction was true. An Austrian force advanced, eighteen thousand strong. Lannes met them upon the field of Montebello. They were strongly posted, with batteries ranged upon the hill sides, which swept the whole plain. It was of the utmost moment that this body should be prevented from combining with the other vast forces of the Austrians. Lannes had but eight thousand men. Could he sustain the unequal conflict for a few hours, Victor, who was some miles in the rear, could come up with a reserve of four thousand men. The French soldiers, fully conscious of the odds against which they were to contend, and of the carnage into the midst of which they were plunging, with shouts of enthusiasm rushed upon their foes. Instantaneously a storm of grape-shot from all the batteries swept through his ranks. Said Lannes, " I could hear the bones crash in my division, like glass in a hail-storm ." For nine long hours, from eleven in the morning till eight at night, the horrid carnage continued. Again and again the mangled, bleeding, wasted columns were rallied to the charge. At last, when three thousand Frenchmen were strewn dead upon the ground, the Austrians broke and fled, leaving also three thousand mutilated corpses and six thousand prisoners behind them. Napoleon, hastening to the aid of his lieutenant, arrived upon the field just in time to see the battle won. He rode up to Lannes. The intrepid soldier stood in the midst of mounds of the dead--his sword dripping with blood in his exhausted hand--his face blackened with powder and smoke--and his uniform soiled and tattered by the long and terrific strife. Napoleon silently, but proudly smiled upon the heroic general, and forgot not his reward. From this battle Lannes received the title of Duke of

Montebello, a title by which his family is distinguished to the present day.

This was the opening of the campaign. It inspired the French with enthusiasm. It nerved the Austrians to despair. Melas now determined to make a desperate effort to break through the toils. Napoleon, with intense solicitude, was watching every movement of his foe, knowing not upon what point the onset would fall. Before day-break in the morning of the 14th of June, Melas, having accumulated forty thousand men, including seven thousand cavalry and two hundred pieces of cannon, made an impetuous assault upon the French, but twenty thousand in number drawn up upon the plain of Marengo. Desaix, with a reserve of six thousand men, was at such a distance, nearly thirty miles from Marengo, that he could not possibly be recalled before the close of the day. The danger was frightful that the French would be entirely cut to pieces, before any succor could arrive. But the quick ear of Desaix caught the sound of the heavy cannonade as it came booming over the plain, like distant thunder. He sprung from his couch and listened. The heavy and uninterrupted roar, proclaimed a pitched battle, and he was alarmed for his beloved chief. Immediately he roused his troops, and they started upon the rush to succor their comrades. Napoleon dispatched courier after courier to hurry the division along, while his troops stood firm through terrific hours, as their ranks were plowed by the murderous discharges of their foes. At last the destruction was too awful for mortal men to endure. Many divisions of the army broke and fled, crying " All is lost--save himself who can ." A scene of frightful disorder ensued. The whole plain was covered with fugitive, swept like an inundation before the multitudinous Austrians. Napoleon still held a few squares together, who slowly and sullenly retreated, while two hundred pieces of artillery, closely pressing them, poured incessant death into their ranks. Every foot of ground was left encumbered with the dead. It was now three o'clock in the afternoon. Melas, exhausted with toil, and assured that he had gained a complete victory, left Gen. Zach to finish the work. He retired to his head quarters, and immediately dispatched couriers all over Europe to announce the great victory of Marengo. Said an Austrian veteran, who had before encountered Napoleon at Arcola and Rivoli, "Melas is too sanguine. Depend upon it our day's work is not yet done. Napoleon will yet be upon us with his reserve."

Just then the anxious eye of the First Consulespied the solid columns of Desaix entering the plain. Desaix, plunging his spurs into his horse, outstripped all the rest, and galloped into the presence of Napoleon. As he cast a glance over the wild confusion and devastation of the field, the exclaimed hurriedly, "I see that the battle is lost. I suppose I can do no more for you than to secure your retreat." "By no means," Napoleon replied with apparently as much composure as if he had been sitting by his own fireside, "the battle, I trust, is gained. Charge with your column. The disordered troops will rally in your rear." Like a rock, Desaix, with his solid phalanx of ten thousand men, met the on-rolling billow of Austrian victory. At the same time Napoleon dispatched an order to Kellerman, with his cavalry, to charge the triumphant column of the Austrians in flank. It was the work of a moment, and the whole aspect of the field was changed. Napoleon rode along the lines of those on the retreat, exclaiming, "My friends, we have retreated far enough. It is now our turn to advance. Recollect that I am in the habit of sleeping on the field of battle." The fugitives, reanimated by the arrival of the reserve, immediately rallied in their rear. The double charge in front and flank was instantly made. The Austrians were checked and staggered. A perfect tornado of bullets from Desaix's division swept their ranks. They poured an answering volley into the bosoms of the French. A bullet pierced the breast of Desaix, and he fell and almost immediately expired. His last words were, "Tell the First Consul that my only regret in dying is, to have perished before having done enough to live in the recollection of posterity." The soldiers, who devotedly loved him, saw his fall, and rushed more madly on to avenge his death. The swollen tide of uproar, confusion, and dismay now turned, and rolled in surging billows in the opposite direction. Hardly one moment elapsed before the Austrians, flushed with victory, found themselves overwhelmed by defeat. In the midst of this terrific scene, an aid rode up to Napoleon and said, "Desaix is dead." But a moment before they were conversing side by side. Napoleon pressed his forehead convulsively with his hand, and exclaimed, mournfully, "Why is it not permitted me to weep! Victory at such a price is dear."

The French now made the welkin ring with shouts of victory. Indescribable dismay filled the Austrian ranks as wildly they rushed before their unrelenting pursuers. Their rout was utter and hopeless. When the sun went down over this field of blood, after twelve hours of the most frightful carnage, a scene was presented horrid enough to appall the heart of a demon. More than twenty thousand human bodies were strewn upon the ground, the dying and the dead, weltering in gore, and in every conceivable form of disfiguration. Horses, with limbs torn their bodies, were struggling in convulsive agonies. Fragments of guns and swords, and of military wagons of every kind were strewed around in wild ruin. Frequent piercing cries, which agony extorted from the lacerated victims of war, rose above the general moanings of anguish, which, like wailings of the storm, fell heavily upon the ear. The shades of night were now descending upon this awful scene of misery. The multitude of the wounded was so great, that notwithstanding the utmost exertions of the surgeons, hour after hour of the long night lingered away, while thousands of the wounded and the dying bit the dust in their agony.

If war has its chivalry and its pageantry, it has also revolting hideousness and demoniac woe. The young, the noble, the sanguine were writhing there in agony. Bullets respect not beauty. They tear out the eye, and shatter the jaw, and rend the cheek, and transform the human face divine into an aspect upon which one can not gaze but with horror. From the field of Marengo many a young man returned to his home so mutilated as no longer to be recognized by friends, and passed a weary life in repulsive deformity. Mercy abandons the arena of battle. The frantic war-horse with iron hoof tramples upon the mangled face, the throbbing and inflamed wounds the splintered bones, and heeds not the shriek of torture. Crushed into the bloody mire by the ponderous wheels of heavy artillery, the victim of barbaric war thinks of mother, and father, and sister, and home, and shrieks, and moans, and dies; his body is stripped by the vagabonds who follow the camp; his naked mangled corpse is covered with a few shovels-full of earth, and left as food for vultures and for dogs and he is forgotten forever--and it is called glory . He who loves war, for the sake of its excitements, its pageantry, and its fancied glory, is the most eminent of all the dupes of folly and of sin. He who loathes war, with inexpressible loathing, who will do everything in his power to avert the dire and horrible calamity, but who will, nevertheless, in the last extremity, with a determined spirit, encounter all its perils, from love of country and of home, who is willing to sacrifice himself and all that is dear to him in life, to promote the well being of his fellow-man, will ever receive the homage of the world, and we also fully believe that he will receive the approval of God. Washington abhorred war in all its forms, yet he braved all its perils.

For the carnage of the field of Marengo, Napoleon can not be held responsible. Upon England and Austria must rest all the guilt of that awful tragedy. Napoleon had done every thing he could do to stop the effusion of blood. He had sacrificed the instincts of pride, in pleading with a haughty foe for peace. His plea was unavailing. Three hundred thousand men were marching upon France to force upon her a detested King. It was not the duty of France to submit to such dictation. Drawing the sword in self-defense, Napoleon fought and conquered. "Te Deum Laudamus."

It is not possible but that Napoleon must have been elated by so resplendent a victory. He knew that Marengo would be classed as the most brilliant of his achievements. The blow had fallen with such terrible severity that the haughty allies were thoroughly humbled. Melas was now at his mercy. Napoleon could dictate peace upon his own terms. Yet he rode over the field of his victory with a saddened spirit, and gazed mournfully upon the ruin and the wretchedness around him. As he was slowly and thoughtfully passing along, through the heaps of the dead with which the ground was encumbered, he met a number of carts, heavily laden with the wounded, torn by balls, and bullets, and fragments of shells, into most hideous spectacles of deformity. As the heavy wheels lumbered over the rough ground, grating the splintered bones, and bruising and opening afresh the inflamed wounds, shrieks of torture were extorted from the victims. Napoleon stopped his horse and uncovered his head, as the melancholy procession of misfortune and woe passed along. Turning to a companion, he said, "We can not but regret not being wounded like these unhappy men, that we might share their sufferings." A more touching expression of sympathy never has been recorded. He who says that this was hypocrisy is a stranger to the generous impulses of a noble heart. This instinctive outburst of emotion never could have been instigated by policy.

Napoleon had fearlessly exposed himself to every peril during this conflict. His clothes were repeatedly pierced by bullets. Balls struck between the legs of his horse, covering him with earth. A cannon-ball took away a piece of the boot from his left leg and a portion of the skin, leaving a scar which was never obliterated.

Before Napoleon Marched for Italy, he had made every effort in his power for the attainment of peace. Now, with magnanimity above all praise, without waiting for the first advance from his conquered foes, he wrote again imploring peace. Upon the field of Marengo, having scattered all his enemies like chaff before him, with the smoke of the conflict still darkening the air, and the groans of the dying swelling upon his ears, laying aside all the formalities of state, with heartfelt feeling and earnestness he wrote to the Emperor of Austria. This extraordinary epistle was thus commenced:

"Sire! It is on the field of battle, amid the sufferings of a multitude of wounded, and surrounded by fifteen thousand corpses, that I beseech your majesty to listen to the voice of humanity, and not to suffer two brave nations to cut each others' throats for interests not their own. It is my part to press this upon your majesty, being upon the very theatre of war. Your majesty's heart can not feel it so keenly as does mine."

The letter was long and most eloquent. "For what are you fighting?" said Napoleon. "For religion? Then make war on the Russians and the English who are the enemies of your faith. Do you wish to guard against revolutionary principles? It is this very war which has extended them over half the Continent, by extending the conquests of France. The continuance of the war can not fail to diffuse them still further. Is it for the balance of Europe? The English threaten that balance far more than does France, for they have become the masters and the tyrants of commerce, and are beyond the reach of resistance. Is it to secure the interests of the house of Austria! Let us then execute the treaty of Campo Formio, which secures to your majesty large indemnities in compensation for the provinces lost in the Netherlands, and secures them to you where you most wish to obtain them, that is, in Italy. Your majesty may send negotiators whither you will, and we will add to the treaty of Campo Formio stipulations calculated to assure you of the continued existence of the secondary states, of all which the French Republic is accused of having shaken. Upon these conditions pace is made, if you will. Let us make the armistice general for all the armies, and enter into negotiations instantly."

A courier was immediately dispatched to Vienna, to convey this letter to the Emperor. In the evening, Bourrienne hastened to congratulate Napoleon upon his extraordinary victory. "What a glorious day!" said Bourrienne. "Yes!" replied Napoleon, mournfully; "very glorious--could I this evening but have embraced Desaix upon the field of battle."

On the same day, and at nearly the same hour in which the fatal bullet pierced the breast of Desaix, an assassin in Egypt plunged a dagger into the bosom of Kleber. The spirits of these illustrious men, these blood-stained warriors, thus unexpectedly met in the spirit-land. There they wander now. How impenetrable the vail which shuts their destiny from our view. The soul longs for clearer vision of that far-distant world, people by the innumerable host of the mighty dead. There Napoleon now dwells. Does he retain his intellectual supremacy? Do his generals gather around him with love and homage! Has his pensive spirit sunk down into gloom and despair, or has it soared into cloudless regions of purity and peace! The mystery of death' Death alone can solve it. Christianity, with its lofty revealings, sheds but dim twilight upon the world off departed spirits. At St. Helena Napoleon said, "Of all the general I ever had under my command Desaix and Kleber possessed the greatest talent. In particular Desaix, as Kleber loved glory only as the means of acquiring wealth and pleasure. Desaix loved glory for itself, and despised every other consideration. To him riches and pleasure were of no value, nor did he ever give them a moment's thought. He was a little black-looking man, about an inch shorter than myself, always badly dressed, sometimes even ragged, and despising alike comfort and convenience. Enveloped in a cloak, Desaix would throw himself under a gun and sleep as contentedly as if reposing in a palace. Luxury had for him no charms. Frank and honest in all his proceedings, he was denominated by the Arabs Sultan the Just. Nature intended him to figure as a consummate general. Kleber and Desaix were irreparable losses to France."

It is impossible to describe the dismay, which pervaded the camp of the Austrians after this terrible defeat. They were entirely cut from all retreat, and were at the mercy of Napoleon. A council of war was held by the Austrian officers during the night, and it was unanimously resolved that capitulation was unavoidable. Early the next morning a flag of truce was sent to the head-quarters of Napoleon. The Austrians offered to abandon Italy, if the generosity of the victor would grant them the boon of not being made prisoners of war. Napoleon met the envoy with great courtesy, and, according to his custom, stated promptly and irrevocably the conditions upon which he was willing to treat. The terms were generous. "The Austrian armies," said he, "may unmolested return to their homes; but all of Italy must be abandoned." Melas, who was eighty years of age, hoped to modify the terms, and again sent the negotiator to suggest some alterations. "Monsieur!" said Napoleon, "my conditions are irrevocable. I did not begin to make war yesterday. Your position is as perfectly comprehended by me as by yourselves. You are encumbered with dead, sick, and wounded, destitute of provisions, deprived of the elite of your army, surrounded on every side, I might exact every thing. But I respect the white hairs of your general, and the valor of your soldiers. I ask nothing but what is rigorously justified by the present position of affairs. Take what steps you may, you will have no other terms." The conditions were immediately signed, and a suspension of arms was agreed upon, until an answer could be received from Vienna.

Napoleon left Paris for this campaign on the 7th of May. The battle of Marengo was fought on the 14th of June. Thus in five weeks Napoleon has scaled the barrier of the Alps: with sixty thousand soldiers, most of them undisciplined recruits, he had utterly discomfited an army of one hundred and twenty thousand men, and regained the whole of Italy. The bosom of every Frenchman throbbed with gratitude and pride. One wild shout of enthusiasm ascended from united France. Napoleon had laid the foundation of his throne deep in the heart of the French nation, and there that foundation still remains unshaken.

Napoleon now entered Milan in triumph. He remained there ten days, busy apparently every hour, by day and by night, in re-organizing the political condition of Italy. The serious and religious tendencies of his mind are developed by the following note, which four days after the battle of Marengo, he wrote to the Consuls in Paris: "To-day, whatever our atheists may say to it, I go in great state to the To Deum which is to be chanted in the Cathedral of Milan. * * The Te Deum , is an anthem of praise, sung in churches on occasion of thanksgiving. It is so called from the first words "Te Deum laudamus," Thee God we praise

An unworthy spirit of detraction has vainly sought to wrest from Napoleon the honor of this victory, and to attribute it all to the flank charge made by Kellerman. Such attempts deserve no detail reply. Napoleon had secretly and suddenly called into being an army, and by its apparently miraculous creation had astounded Europe. He had effectually deceived the vigilance of his enemies, so as to leave them entirely in the dark respecting his point of attack. He had conveyed that army with all its stores, over the pathless crags of the Great St. Bernard. Like an avalanche he had descended from the mountains upon the plains of startled Italy. He had surrounded the Austrian hosts, though they were doubled his numbers, with a net through which they could not break. In a decisive battle he had scattered their ranks before him, like chaff by the whirlwind. He was nobly seconded by those generals whom his genius had chosen and created. It is indeed true, that without his generals and his soldiers he could not have gained the victory. Massena contributed to the result by his matchless defense of Genoa; Moreau, by holding in abeyance the army of the Rhine; Lannes, by his iron firmness on the plain of Montebello; Desaix, by the promptness with which he rushed to the rescue, as soon as his car caught the far-off thunders of the cannon of Marengo; and Kellerman, by his admirable flank charge of cavalry. But it was the genius of Napoleon which planned the mighty combination, which roused and directed the enthusiasm of the generals, which inspired the soldiers with fearlessness and nerved them for the strife, and which, through these efficient agencies, secured the astounding results.

Napoleon established his triumphant army, now increased to eighty thousand men, in the rich valley of the Po. He assigned to the heroic Massena the command of this triumphant host, and ordering all the forts and citadels which blocked the approaches from France to be blown up, set out, on the 24th of June, for his return to Paris. In re-crossing the Alps, by the pass of Mt. Cenis, he met the carriage of Madame Kellerman, who was going to Italy to join her husband. Napoleon ordered his carriage to be stopped, and alighting, greeted the lady with great courtesy, and congratulated her upon the gallant conduct of her husband at Marengo. As he was riding along one day, Bourrienne spoke of the world-wide renown which the First Consul had attained.

"Yes," Napoleon thoughtfully replied. "A few more events like this campaign, and my name may perhaps go down to posterity."

"I think," Bourrienne rejoined, "that you have already done enough to secure a long and lasting fame."

"Done enough!" Napoleon replied. "You are very good! It is true that in less than two years I have conquered Cairo, Paris, Milan. But were I to die to-morrow, half a page of general history would be all that would be devoted to my exploits."

Napoleon's return to Paris, through the provinces of France, was a scene of constant triumph. The joy of the people amounted almost to frenzy. Bonfires, illuminations, the pealing of bells, and the thunders of artillery accompanied him all the way. Long lines of young maidens, selected for their grace and beauty, formed avenues of loveliness and smiles through which he was to pass, and carpeted his path with flowers. He arrived in Paris at midnight the 2d of July, having been absent but eight weeks.

The enthusiasm of the Parisians was unbounded and inexhaustible. Day after day, and night after night, the festivities continued. The Palace of the Tuileries was ever thronged with a crowd, eager to catch a glimpse of the preserver of France. All the public bodies waited upon him with congratulations. Bells rung, cannon thundered, bonfires and illuminations blazed, rockets and fire-works, in meteoric splendor filled the air, bands of music poured forth their exuberant strains, and united Paris, thronging the garden of the Tuileries and flooding back into the Elysian Fields, rent the heavens with deafening shouts of exultation. As Napoleon stood at the window of his palace, witnessing this spectacle of a nation's gratitude, he said, "The sound of these acclamations is as sweet to me, as the voice of Josephine. How happy I am to be beloved by such a people." Preparations were immediately made for a brilliant and imposing solemnity in commemoration of the victory. "Let no triumphal arch be raised to me," said Napoleon. "I wish for no triumphal arch but the public satisfaction."

It is not strange that enthusiasm and gratitude should have glowed in the ardent bosoms of the French. In four months Napoleon had raised France from an abyss of ruin to the highest pinnacle of prosperity and renown. For anarchy he had substituted law, for bankruptcy a well-replenished treasury, for ignominious defeat resplendent victory, for universal discontent as universal satisfaction. The invaders were driven from France, the hostile alliance broken, and the blessings of peace were now promised to the war-harassed nation.

During this campaign there was presented a very interesting illustration of Napoleon's wonderful power of anticipating the progress of coming events. Bourrienne, one day, just before the commencement of the campaign, entered the cabinet at the Tuileries, and found an immense map of Italy, unrolled upon the carpet, and Napoleon stretched upon it. With pins, whose heads were tipped with red and black sealing-wax, to represent the French and Austrian forces, Napoleon was studying all the possible combinations and evolutions of the two hostile armies. Bourrienne, in silence, but with deep interest, watched the progress of this pin campaign. Napoleon, having arranged the pins with red heads, where he intended to conduct the French troops, and with the black pins designating the point which he supposed the Austrians would occupy, looked up to his secretary, and said:

"Do you think that I shall beat Melas?"

"Why, how can I tell!" Bourrienne answered.

"Why, you simpleton," said Napoleon, playfully; "just look here. Melas is at Alexandria, where he has his head-quarters. He will remain there until Genoa surrenders. He has in Alexandria his magazines, his hospitals, his artillery, his reserves. Passing the Alps here," sticking a pin into the Great St. Bernard, "I fall upon Melas in his rear; I cut off his communications with Austria. I meet him here in the valley of the Bormida." So saying, he stuck a red pin into the plain of Marengo.

Bourrienne regarded this maneuvering of pins as mere pastime. His countenance expressed his perfect incredulity. Napoleon, perceiving this, addressed to him some of his usual apostrophes, in which he was accustomed playfully to indulge in moments of relaxation, such as, You ninny, You goose; and rolled up the map. Ten weeks passed away, and Bourrienne found himself upon the banks of the Bormida, writing, at Napoleon's dictation, an account of the battle of Marengo. Astonished to find Napoleon's anticipations thus minutely fulfilled, he frankly avowed his admiration of the military sagacity thus displayed. Napoleon himself smiled at the justice of his foresight.

Two days before the news of the battle of Marengo arrived in Vienna, England effected a new treaty with Austria, for the more vigorous prosecution of the war. By this convention it was provided that England should loan Austria ten millions of dollars, to bear no interest during the continuance of the conflict. And the Austrian cabinet bound itself not to make peace with France, without the consent of the Court of St. James. The Emperor of Austria was now sadly embarrassed. His sense of honor would not allow him to violate his pledge to the King of England, and to make peace. On the other hand, he trembled at the thought of seeing the armies of the invincible Napoleon again marching upon his capital. He, therefore, resolved to temporize, and, in order to gain time, sent an embassador to Paris. The plenipotentiary presented to Napoleon a letter, in which the Emperor stated, "You will give credit to every thing which Count Julien shall say on my part. I will ratify whatever he shall do." Napoleon, prompt in action, and uniformed of the new treaty between Ferdinand and George III., immediately caused the preliminaries of peace to be drawn up, which were signed by the French and Austrian ministers. The cabinet in Vienna, angry with their embassador for not protracting the discussion, refused to ratify the treaty, recalled Count Julien, sent him into exile, informed the First Consul of the treat which bound Austria not to make peace without the concurrence of Great Britain, assured France of the readiness of the English Cabinet to enter into negotiations, and urged the immediate opening of a Congress at Luneville, to which plenipotentiaries should be sent from each of the three great contending powers. Napoleon was highly indignant in view of this duplicity and perfidy. Yet, controlling his anger, he consented to treat with England, and with that view proposed a naval armistice , with the mistress of the seas. To this proposition England peremptorily refused to accede, as it would enable France to throw supplies into Egypt and Malta, which island England was besieging. The naval armistice would have been undeniably for the interests of France. But the continental armistice was as undeniably adverse to her interests, enabling Austria to recover from her defeats, and to strengthen her armies. Napoleon, fully convinced that England, in he[r inaccessible position, did not wish for peace, and that her only object, in endeavoring to obtain admittance to the Congress, was that she might throw obstacles in the way of reconciliation with Austria, offered to renounce all armistice with England, and to treat with her separately. This England also refused.

It was now September. Two months had passed in these vexations and sterile negotiations. Napoleon had taken every step in his power to secure peace. He sincerely desired it. He had already won all the laurels he could wish to win on the field of battle. The reconstruction of society in France, and the consolidation of his power, demanded all his energies. The consolidation of his power! That was just what the government of England dreaded. The consolidation of democratic power in France was dangerous to king and to noble. William Pits, the soul of the aristocratic government of England, determined still to prosecute the war. France could not harm England. But England, with her invincible fleet, could sweep the commerce of France from the seas. Fox and his coadjutors with great eloquence and energy opposed the war. Their efforts were, however, unavailing. The people of England, notwithstanding all the efforts of the government to defame the character of the First Consul, still cherished the conviction that, after all, Napoleon was their friend. Napoleon, in subsequent years, while reviewing these scenes of his early conflicts, with characteristic eloquence and magnanimity, gave utterance to the following sentiments which, it is as certain as destiny, that the verdict of the world will yet confirm.

"Pitt was the master of European policy. He held in his hands the moral fate of nations. But he made an ill use of his power. He kindled the fire of discord throughout the universe; and his name, like that of Erostratus, will be inscribed in history, amidst flames, lamentations, and tears. Twenty-five years of universal conflagration; the numerous coalitions that added fuel to the flame; the revolution and devastation of Europe; the bloodshed of nations; the frightful debt of England, by which all these horrors were maintained; the pestilential system of loans, by which the people of Europe are oppressed; the general discontent that now prevails--all must be attributed to Pitt. Posterity will brand him as a scourge. The man so lauded in his own time, will hereafter be regarded as the genius of evil. Not that I consider him to have been willfully atrocious, or doubt his having entertained the conviction that he was acting right. But St. Bartholomew had also its conscientious advocates. The Pope and cardinals celebrated it by a Te Deum ; and we have no reason to doubt their having done so in perfect sincerity. Such is the weakness of human reason and judgment! But that for which posterity will, above all, execrate the memory of Pitt, is the hateful school, which he has left behind him; its insolent Machiavelism, its profound immorality, its cold egotism, and its utter disregard of justice and human happiness. Whether it be the effect of admiration and gratitude, or the result of mere instinct and sympathy, Pitt is, and will continue to be, the idol of the European aristocracy. There was, indeed, a touch of the Sylla in his character. His system has kept the popular cause in check, and brought about the triumph of the patricians. As for Fox, one must not look for his model among the ancients. He is himself a model, and his principles will sooner or later rule the world. The death of Fox was one of the fatalities of my career. Had his life been prolonged, affairs would taken a totally different turn. The cause of the people would have triumphed, and we should have established a new order of things in Europe."

Austria really desired peace. The march of Napoleon's armies upon Vienna was an evil more to be dreaded than even the consolidation of Napoleon's power in France. But Austria was, by loans and treaties, so entangled with England, that she could make not peace without the consent of the Court of St. James. Napoleon found that he was but triffled with. Interminable difficulties were thrown in the way of negotiation. Austria was taking advantage of the cessation of hostilities, merely to recruit her defeated armies, that, soon as the approaching winter had passed away, she might fall, with renovated energies, upon France. The month of November had now arrived, and the mountains, whitened with snow, were swept by the bleak winds of winter. The period of the armistice had expired. Austria applied for its prolongation. Napoleon was no longer thus to be duped. He consented, however, to a continued suspension of hostilities, on condition that the treaty of peace were signed within forty-eight hours. Austria, believing that no sane man would march an army into Germany in the dead of winter, and that she should have abundant time to prepare for a spring campaign, refused. The armies of France were immediately on the move. The Emperor of Austria had improved every moment of this transient interval of peace, in recruiting his forces. In person he had visited the army to inspire his troops with enthusiasm. The command of the imperial forces was intrusted to his second brother, the Archduke John. Napoleon moved with his accustomed vigor. The political necessities of Paris and of France rendered it impossible for him to leave the metropolis. He ordered one powerful army, under General Brune, to attack the Austrians in Italy, on the banks of Mincio, and to press firmly toward Vienna. In the performance of this operation, General Macdonald, in the dead of winter, effected his heroic passage over the Alps by the pass of the Splugen. Victory followed their standards.

Moreau, with his magnificent army, commenced a winter campaign on the Rhine. Between the rivers Iser and Inn there is an enormous forest, many leagues in extent, of sombre firs and pines. It is a dreary and almost uninhabited wilderness, of wild ravines, and tangled under-brush. Two great roads have been cut through the forest, and sundry woodmen's paths penetrate it at different points. In the centre there is a little hamlet, of a few miserable huts, called Hohenlinden. In this forest, on the night of the 3d of December, 1800, Moreau, with sixty thousand men, encountered the Archduke John with seventy thousand Austrian troops. The clocks upon the towers of Munich had but just tolled the hour of midnight when both armies were in motion, each hoping to surprise the other. A dismal wintry storm was howling over the tree tops, and the smothering snow, falling rapidly, obliterated all traces of a path, and rendered it almost impossible to drag through the drifts the ponderous artillery. Both parties, in the dark and tempestuous night, became entangled in the forest, and the heads of their columns in various places met. An awful scene of confusion, conflict, and carnage then ensued. Imagination can not compass the terrible sublimity of that spectacle. The dark midnight, the howlings of the wintry storm, the driving sheets of snow, the incessant roar of artillery and of musketry from one hundred and thirty thousand combatants, the lightning flashes of the guns, the crash of the falling trees as the heavy cannon-balls swept through the forest, the floundering of innumerable horsemen bewildered in the pathless snow, the shout of onset, the shriek of death, and the burst of martial music from a thousand bands--all combined to present a scene of horror and of demoniac energy, which probably even this lost world never presented before. The darkness of the black forest was so intense, and the snow fell in flakes so thick and fast and blinding, that the combatants could with difficulty see each other. They often judged of the foe only by his position, and fired at the flashes gleaming through the gloom. At times, hostile divisions became intermingled in inextricable confusion, and hand to hand, bayonet crossing bayonet, and sword clashing against sword, they fought with the ferocity of demons; for though the officers of an army may be influenced by the most elevated sentiments of dignity and of honor, the mass of the common soldiers have ever been the most miserable, worthless, and degraded of mankind. As the advancing and retreating host wavered to and fro, the wounded, by thousands, were left on hill-sides and in dark ravines, with the drifting snow, crimsoned with blood, their only blanket; there in solitude and agony to moan and freeze and die. What death-scenes the eye of God must have witnessed that night, in the solitudes of that dark, tempest-tossed, and blood-stained forest! At last the morning dawned through the unbroken clouds, and the battle raged with renovated fury. Nearly twenty thousand mutilated bodies of the dead and wounded were left upon the field, with gory locks frozen to their icy pillows, and covered with mounds of snow. At last the French were victorious at every point. The Austrians, having lost twenty-five thousand men in killed, wounded, and prisoners, one hundred pieces of artillery, and an immense number of wagons, fled in dismay. This terrific conflict has been immortalized by the noble epic of Campbell, which is now familiar wherever the English language is known.

"On Linden, when the sun was low, All bloodless lay the untrodden snow, And dark as winter was the flow Or Iser, rolling rapidly. "But Linden saw another sight, When the drums beat at dead of night, Commanding fires of death to light The darkness of her scenery." &c.

The retreating Austrians rushed down the valley of the Danube. Moreau followed thundering at their heels, plunging balls and shells into their retreating ranks. The victorious French were within thirty miles of Vienna, and the capital was in a state of indescribable dismay. The Emperor again sent imploring an armistice. The application was promptly acceded to, for Napoleon was contending only for peace. Yet with unexempled magnanimity, notwithstanding these astonishing victories, Napoleon made no essential alterations in his terms. Austria was at his feet. His conquering armies were almost in sight of the steeples of Vienna. There was no power which the Emperor could present to obstruct their resistless march. He might have exacted any terms of humiliation. But still he adhered to the first terms which he had proposed. Moreau was urged by some of his officers to press on to Vienna. "We had better halt," he replied, "and be content with peace. It is for that alone that we are fighting." The Emperor of Austria was thus compelled to treat without the concurrence of England. The insurmountable obstacle in the way of peace was thus removed. At Luneville, Joseph Bonaparte appeared as the embassador of Napoleon, and Count Cobentzel as the plenipotentiary of Austria. The terms of the treaty were soon settled, and France was again at peace with all the world, England alone excepted. By this treaty the Rhine was acknowledged as the boundary of France. The Adige limited the possessions of Austria in Italy; and Napoleon made it an essential article that every Italian imprisoned in the dungeons of Austria for political offences, should immediately be liberated. There was to be no interference by either with the new republics which had sprung up in Italy. They were to be permitted to choose whatever form of government they preferred. In reference to this treaty, Sir Walter Scott makes the candid admission that "the treaty of Luneville was not much more advantageous to France than that of Campo Formio. The moderation of the First Consul indicated at once his desire for peace upon the Continent, and considerable respect for the bravery and strength of Austria." And Alison, in cautious but significant phrase, remarks, "These conditions did not differ materially from those offered by Napoleon before the renewal of the war; a remarkable circumstance , when it is remembered how vast and addition the victories of Marengo, Hohenlinden, and the Mincio, had since made to the preponderance of the French armies."

It was, indeed, "a remarkable circumstance," that Napoleon should have manifested such unparalleled moderation, under circumstances of such aggravated indignity. In Napoleon's first Italian campaign he was contending solely for peace. At last he attained it, in the treaty of Campo Formio, on terms equally honorable to Austria and to France. On his return from Egypt, he found the armies of Austria, three hundred thousand strong, in alliance with England, invading the territories of the Republic. He implored peace, in the name of bleeding humanity, upon the fair basis of the treaty of Campo Formio. His foes regarded his supplication as the imploring cry of weakness, and treated it with scorn. With new vigor they poured their tempests of balls and shells upon France. Napoleon sealed the Alps, and dispersed his foes at Marengo, like autumn leaves before the Alps, and dispersed his foes at Marengo, like autumn leaves before the gale. Amid the smoke and the blood and the groans of the field of his victory, he again wrote imploring peace; and he wrote in terms dictated by the honest and gushing sympathies of a humane man, and not in the cold and stately forms of the diplomatist. Crushed as his foes were, he rose not in his demands, but nobly said, "I am still willing to make peace upon the fair basis of the treaty of Campo Formio." His treacherous foes, to gain time to recruit their armies, that they might fall upon him with renovated vigor, agreed to an armistice. They then threw all possible embarrassments in the way of negotiation, and prolonged the armistice till the winds of winter were sweeping fiercely over the snow-covered hills of Austria. They thought that it was then too late for Napoleon to make any movements until spring, and that they had a long winter before them, in which to prepare for another campaign. They refused peace. Through storms and freezing gales and drifting snows the armies of Napoleon marched painfully to Hohenlinden. The hosts of Austria were again routed, and were swept away, as the drifted snow flies before the gale. Ten thousand Frenchmen lie cold in death, the terrible price of the victory. The Emperor of Austria, in his palaces, heard the thunderings of Napoleon's approaching artillery. He implored peace. "It is all that I desire," said Napoleon; "I am not fighting for ambition or for conquest. I am still ready to make peace upon the fair basis of the treaty of Campo Formio."

While all the Continent was now at peace with France, England alone, with indomitable resolution, continued the war, without allies, and without any apparent or avowed object. France, comparatively powerless upon the seas, could strike no blows which would be felt by the distant islanders. "On every point," says Sir Walter Scott, "the English squadrons annihilated the commerce of France, crippled her revenues, and blockaded her forts." The treaty of Luneville was signed the 9th of February, 1801. Napoleon lamenting, the continued hostility of England, in announcing this peace to the people of France, remarked, "Why is not this treaty the treaty of a general peace? This was the wish of France. This has been the constant object of the efforts of her government. But its desires are fruitless. All Europe knows that the British minister has endeavored to frustrate the negotiations at Luneville. In vain was it declared to him that France was ready to enter into a separate negotiation.

This declaration only produced a refusal under the pretext that England could not abandon her ally. Since then, when that ally consented to treat without England, that government sought other means to delay a peace so necessary to the world. It raises pretensions contrary to the dignity and rights of all nations. The whole commerce of Asia, and of immense colonies, does not satisfy its ambition. All the seas must submit to the exclusive sovereignty of England." As William Pitt received the tidings of this discomfiture of his allies, in despairing despondency, he exclaimed, "Fold up the map of Europe. In need not again be opened for twenty years."

While these great affairs were in progress, Napoleon, in Paris, was consecrating his energies with almost miraculous power, in developing all the resources of the majestic empire under his control. He possessed the power of abstraction to a degree which has probably never been equaled. He could concentrate all his attention for any length of time upon one subject, and then, laying that aside entirely, without expending any energies in unavailing anxiety, could turn to another, with all the freshness and the vigor of an unpreoccupied mind. Incessant mental labor was the luxury of his life. "Occupation," said he, "is my element. I am born and made for it. I have found the limits beyond which I could not use my legs. I have seen the extent to which I could use my eyes. But I have never known any bounds to my capacity for application."

The universality of Napoleon's genius was now most conspicuous. The revenues of the nation were replenished, and all the taxes arranged to the satisfaction of the people. The Bank of France was reorganized, and new energy infused into its operations. Several millions of dollars were expended in constructing and perfecting five magnificent roads radiating from Paris to the frontiers of the empire. Robbers, the vagabonds of disbanded armies, infested the roads, rendering traveling dangerous in the extreme. "Be patient," said Napoleon. "Give me a month or two. I must first conquer peace abroad. I will then do speedy and complete justice upon these highwaymen." A very important canal, connecting Belgium with France, had been commenced some years before. The engineers could not agree respecting the best direction of the cutting through the highlands which separated the valley of the Oise from that of the Somme. He visited the spot in person: decided the question promptly, and decided it wisely, and the canal was pressed to its completion. He immediately caused three new bridges to be thrown across the Seine at Paris. He commenced the magnificent road of the Simplon, crossing the rugged Alps with a broad and smooth highway, which for ages will remain a durable monument of the genius and energy of Napoleon. In gratitude for the favors he had received from the monks of the Great St. Bernard, he founded two similar establishments for the aid of travelers, one on Mount Cenis, the other on the Simplon, and both auxiliary to the convent on the Great St. Bernard. Concurrently with these majestic undertakings, he commenced the compilation of the civil code of France. The ablest lawyers of Europe were summoned to this enterprise, and the whole work was discussed section by section in the Council of State, over which Napoleon presided. The lawyers were amazed to find that the First Consul was as perfectly familiar with all the details of legal and political science, as he was with military strategy.

Bourrienne mentions, that one day, a letter was received from an emigrant, General Durosel, who had taken refuge in the island of Jersey. The following is an extract from the letter:

"You can not have forgotten, general, that when your late father was obliged to take your brothers from the college of Autun, he was unprovided with money, and asked of me one hundred and twenty-five dollars, which I lent him with pleasure. After his return, he had not an opportunity of paying me, and when I left Ajaccio, your mother offered to dispose of some plate, in order to pay the debt. To this I objected, and told her that I would wait until she could pay me at her convenience. Previous to the Revolution, I believe that it was not in her power to fulfill her wish of discharging the debt. I am sorry to be obliged to trouble you about such a trifle. But such is my unfortunate situation, that even this trifle is of some importance to me. At the age of eighty-six, general, after having served my country for sixty years, I am compelled to take refuge here, and to subsist on a scanty allowance, granted by the English government to French emigrants. I say emigrants , for I am obliged to be one against my will."

Upon hearing this letter read, Napoleon immediately and warmly said, "Bourrienne, this is sacred. Do not lose a moment. Send the old man ten times the sum. Write to General Durosel, that he shall immediately be erased from the list of emigrants. What mischief those brigands of the Convention have done. I can never repair it all." Napoleon uttered these words with a degree of emotion which he had rarely before evinced. In the evening he inquired, with much interest of Bourrienne, if he had executed his orders.

Many attempts were made at this time to assassinate the First Consul. Though France, with the most unparalleled unanimity surrounded him with admiration, gratitude, and homage, there were violent men in the two extremes of society, among the Jacobins and the inexorable Royalists, who regarded him as in their way. Napoleon's escape from the explosion of the infernal machine, got up by the Royalists, was almost miraculous.

On the evening of the 24th of December, Napoleon was going to the Opera, to hear Haydn's Oratorio of the Creation, which was to be performed for the first time. Intensely occupied by business, he was reluctant to go; but to gratify Josephine, yielded to her urgent request. It was necessary for his carriage to pass through a narrow street. A cart, apparently by accident overturned, obstructed the passage. A barrel suspended beneath the cart, contained as deadly a machine as could be constructed with gun-powder and all the missiles of death. The coachman succeeded in forcing his way by the cart. He had barely passed when an explosion took place, which was all over Paris, and which seemed to shake the city to its foundations. Eight persons were instantly killed, and more than sixty were wounded, of whom about twenty subsequently died. The houses for a long distance, on each side of the street, were fearfully shattered, and many of them were nearly blown to pieces. The carriage rocked as upon the billows of the sea, and the windows were shattered to fragments. Napoleon had been in too many scenes of terror to be alarmed by any noise or destruction which gunpowder could produce. "Ha!" said he, with perfect composure; "we are blown up." One of his companions in the carriage, greatly terrified, thrust his head through the demolished window, and called loudly to the driver to stop. "No, no!" said Napoleon; "drive on." When the First Consul entered the Opera House, he appeared perfectly calm and unmoved. The greatest consternation, however, prevailed in all parts of the house, for the explosion had been heard, and the most fearful apprehensions were felt for the safety of the idolized Napoleon. As soon as he appeared, thunders of applause, which shook the very walls of the theatre, gave affecting testimony of the attachment of the people to his person. In a few moments, Josephine, who had come in her private carriage, entered the box. Napoleon turned to her with perfect tranquillity, and said, "The rascals tried to blow me up. Where is the book of the Oratorio?"

Napoleon soon left the Opera and returned to the Tuileries. He found a vast crowd assembled there, attracted by affection for his person, and anxiety for his safety. The atrocity of this attempt excited universal horror, and only increased the already almost boundless popularity of the First Consul. Deputations and addresses were immediately poured in upon him from Paris and from all the departments of France, congratulating him upon his escape. It was at first thought that this conspiracy was the work of the Jacobins. There were in Paris more than a hundred of the leaders of the execrable party, who had obtained a sanguinary notoriety during the reign of terror. They were active members of a Jacolin Club, a violent and vulgar gathering continually plotting the overthrow of the government, and the assassination of the First Consul. They were thoroughly detested by the people, and the community was glad to avail itself of any plausible pretext for banishing them from France. Without sufficient evidence that they were actually guilty of this particular outrage, in the strong excitement and indignation of the moment a decree was passed by the legislative bodies, sending one hundred and sixty of these bloodstained culprits into exile. The wish was earnestly expressed that Napoleon would promptly punish them by his own dictatorial power. Napoleon had, in fact, acquired such unbounded popularity, and the nation was so thoroughly impressed with a sense of his justice, and his wisdom, the whatever he said was done. He, however, insisted that the business should be conducted by the constituted tribunals and under the regular forms of law.

"The responsibility of this measure," said Napoleon, "must rest with the legislative body. The consuls are irresponsible. But the ministers are not. Any one of them who should sign an arbitrary decree, might hereafter be called to account. Not a single individual must be compromised. The consuls themselves know not what may happen. As for me, while I live, I am not afraid that any one will be killed, and then I can not answer for the safety of my two colleagues. It would be your turn to govern," said, he, smiling, and turning to Cambaceres;" and you are not as yet very firm in the stirrups . It will be better to have a law for the present, as well as for the future." It was finally, after much deliberation, decided that the Council of State should draw up a declaration of the reasons, for the act. The First Consul was to sign the decree, and the Senate was to declare whether it was or was not constitutional. Thus cautiously Napoleon proceed under circumstances so exciting. The law, however, was unjust and tyrannical. Guilty as these men were of other crimes, by which they had forfeited all sympathy, it subsequently appeared that they were not guilty of this crime. Napoleon was evidently embraced by this uncertainty of their guilty, and was not willing that they should be denounced as contrivers of the infernal machine. "We believe ," said he, "that they are guilty. But we do not know it. They must be transported for the crimes which they have committed, the massacres and the conspiracies already proved against them." The decree was passed. But Napoleon, strong in popularity, became so convinced of the powerlessness and insignificance of these Jacobins, that the decree was never enforced against them. They remained in France. But they were conscious that the eye of the police was upon them. "It is not my own person," said Napoleon, "that I seek to avenge. My fortune which has preserved me so often on the field of battle, will continue to preserve me. I think not of myself. I think of social order which it is my mission to re-establish, and of the national honor, which it is my duty to purge from an abominable stain." To the innumerable addresses of congratulation and attachment which this occurrence elicited Napoleon replied. "I have been touched by the proofs of affection which the people of Paris have shown me on this occasion. I deserve them. For the only aim of my thoughts, and of my actions, is to augment the prosperity and the glory of France. While those banditti confined themselves to direct attacks upon me, I could leave to the laws the task of punishing them. But since they have endangered the population of the capital by a crime, unexampled in history, the punishment must be equally speedy and terrible."

It was soon proved, much to the surprise of Napoleon, that the atrocious act was perpetrated by the partisans of the Bourbons. Many of the most prominent of the Loyalists were implicated in this horrible conspiracy. Napoleon felt that he deserved their gratitude. He had interposed to save them from the fury of the Jacobins. Against the remonstrances of his friends, he had passed a decree which restored one hundred and fifty thousand of these wandering emigrants to France. He had done every thing in his power to enable them to regain their confiscated estates. He had been in all respects their friend and benefactor, and he would not believe, until the proof was indisputable, that they could thus requite him. The wily Fouche, however, dragged the whole matter into light. The prominent conspirators were arrested and shot. The following letter, written on this occasion by Josephine, to the Minister of Police, strikingly illustrates the benevolence of her heart, and exhibits in a very honorable light the character of Napoleon.

"While I yet tremble at the frightful event which has just occurred, I am distressed through fear of the punishment to be inflicted on the guilty, who belong, it is said, to families with whom I once lived in habits of intercourse. I shall be solicited by mothers, sisters, and disconsolate wives, and my heart will be broken through my inability to obtain all the mercy for which I would plead. I know that the clemency of the First who belong, it is said, to families with whom I once lived in habits of intercourse. I shall be solicited by mothers,sisters, and disconsolate wives, and my heart will be broken through my inability to obtain all the mercy for which I would plead. I know that the clemency of the First Consul is great--his attachment to me extreme. The chief of the government has not been alone exposed; and it is that which will render him severe, inflexible. I conjure you, therefore, to do all in your power to prevent inquiries being pushed too far. Do not detect all those persons who have been accomplices in this odious transaction. Let not France, so long overwhelmed in consternation, by public executions, groan anew, beneath such inflictions. When the ringleaders of this nefarious attempt shall have been secured, let severity give place to pity for inferior agents, seduced, as they may have been by dangerous falsehoods or exaggerated opinions. As a woman, a wife, and a mother, I must feel the heartrendings of those will apply to me. Act, citizen minister, in such a way that the number of these may be lessened."

It seems almost miraculous that Napoleon should have escaped the innumerable conspiracies which at this time were formed against him. The partisans of the Bourbons though that if Napoleon could be removed, the Bourbons might regain their throne. It was his resistless genius alone, which enabled France to triumph over combined Europe. His death would leave France without a leader. The armies of the allies could then, with bloody strides, march to Paris, and place the hated Bourbons on the throne. France knew this, and adored its preserver. Monarchical Europe knew this, and hence all the engergies of its combined kings were centred upon Napoleon. More than thirty of these consipracies were detected by the police. London was the hot-house where they were engendered. Air-guns were aimed to Napoleon. Assassins dogged him with their poniards. A bomb-shell was invented, weighing about fifteen pounds, which was to be thrown in at his carriage-window, and which exploding by its own concussion, would hurl death on every side. The conspirators were perfectly reckless of the lives of others, if they could only destroy the life of Napoleon. The agents of the infernal-machine had the barbarity to get a young girl fifteen years of age to hold the horse who drew the machine. This was to disarm suspicion. The poor child was blown into such fragments, that no part of her body. excepting the feet, could afterwards be found. At last Napoleon became aroused, and declared that he would "teach those Bourbons that he was not a man to be shot at like a dog."

One day at St. Helena, as he was putting on his flannel waistcoat, he observed Las Casas looking at him very steadfastly.

"Well! what is your Excellency thinking of?" said Napoleon, with a smile.

"Sire," Las Casas replied, "in a pamphlet which I lately read, I found it stated that your majesty was shielded by a coat-of-mail, for the security of your person. I was thinking that I could bear positive evidence that at St. Helena at least, all precautions for personal safety have been laid aside."

"This," said Napoleon, "is one of the thousand absurdities which have just mentioned is the more ridiculous, since every individual about me well knows how careless I am with regard to self-preservation. Accustomed from the age of eighteen to be exposed to the connon-ball, and knowing the inutility of precautions, I abandoned myself to my fate. When I came to the head of affairs, I might still have fancied myself surrounded by the dangers of the field of battle; and I might have regarded the conspiracies which were formed against me as so many bomb-shells. But I followed my old course. I trusted to my lucky star, and left all precautions to the police. I was perhaps the only sovereign in Europe who dispensed with a body-guard. Every one could freely approach me, without having, as it were, to pass through military barracks. Maria Lousia was much astonished to see me so poorly guarded, and she often remarked that her father was surrounded by bayonets. For my part, I had no better defense at the Tuileries than I have here. I do not even know where to find my sword," said he, looking around the room; "do you see it? I have, to be sure, incurred great dangers. Upward of thirty plots were found against me. These have been proved by authentic testimony, without mentioning many which never came to light. Some sovereigns invent conspiracies against themselves; for my part, I made it a rule carefully to conceal them whenever I could. The crisis most serious to me was during the interval from the battle of Marengo, to the attempt of George Cadoudal and the affair of the Duke D'Enghien"

Napoleon now, with his accustomed vigor, took hold of the robbers an and made short work with them. The insurgent armies of La Vendee, numbering more than one hundred thousand men, and filled with adventurers and desperadoes of every kind, were disbanded when their chiefs yielded homage to Napoleon. Many of these men, accustomed to banditti warfare, took to the highways. The roads were so infested by them, that travailing became exceedingly perilous, and it was necessary that every stage-coach which left Paris should be accompanied by a guard of armed soldiers. To remedy a state of society thus convulsed to its very centre, special tribunals were organized, consisting of eight judges. They were to take cognizance of all such crimes as conspiracies, robberies, and acts of violence of any kind. The armed bands of Napoleon swept over France like a whirlwind. The robbers were seized, tried, and shot without delay. Order was at once restored. The people thought not of the dangerous power they were placing in the hands of the First Consul. They asked only for a commander, who was able and willing to quell the tumult of the times. Such a commander they found in Napoleon. They were more than willing to confer upon him all the power he could desire. "You know what is best for us;"" said the people of Napoleon. "Direct us what to do, and we will do it." It was thus that absolute power came voluntarily into his hands. Under the circumstances it was so natural that it can excite no suspicion. He was called First Consul. But he already swayed a scepter more mighty than that of the Caesars. But sixteen months had now elapsed since Napoleon landed at Frejus. In that time he had attained the throne of France. He had caused order and prosperity to emerge from the chaos of revolution. By his magnanimity he had disarmed Russia, by his armies had humbled Austria, and had compelled continental Europe to accept an honorable peace. He merited the gratitude of his countrymen, and he received it in overflowing measure. Through all these incidents, so eventful and so full of difficulty, it is not easy to point to a single act of Napoleon, which indicates a malicious or an ungenerous spirit.

"I fear nothing," said Napoleon at St. Helena, "for my renown. Posterity will do me justice. It will compare the good which I have done with faults which I have committed. If I had succeeded I should have died with the reputation of being the greatest man who ever existed. From being nothing I became, by my own exertions, the most powerful monarch of the universe, without committing any crime. My ambition was great, but it rested on the opinion of the masses. I have always thought that sovereignty resides in the people. The empire, as I had organized it, was but a great republic. Called to the throne by the voice of the people, my maxim has always been a career open to talent without distinction of birth . It is for this system of equality that the European oligarchy detests me. And yet in England talent and great services raise a man to the highest rank. England should have understood me."

The French Revolution," said Napoleon, "was a general movement of the mass of the nation against the privileged classes. The nobles were exempt from the burdens of the state, and yet exclusively occupied all the posts of honor and emolument. The revolution destroyed these exclusive privileges, and established equality of rights. All the avenues of wealth and greatness were equally open to every citizen, according to his talents. The French nation established the imperial throne, and placed me upon it. The throne of France was granted before to Hugh Capet, by a few bishops and nobles. The imperial throne was given to me, by the desire of the people."

Joseph Bonaparte was of very essential service to Napoleon in the diplomatic intercourse of the times. Lucien also was employed in various ways, and the whole family were taken under the protection of the First Consul. At St. Helena Napoleon uttered the following graphic and truthful eulogium upon his brothers and sisters: "What family, in similar circumstances, would have acted better? Every one is not qualified to be a statesman. That requires a combination of powers which does not often fall to the lot of any one. In this respect all my brothers were singularly situated; they possessed at once too much and too little talent. They felt themselves too strong to resign themselves. blindly to a guiding counselor, and yet too weak to be left entirely to themselves. But take them all in all I have certainly good reason to be proud of my family. Joseph would have been an honor to society in any country, and Lucien would have been an honor to any assembly; Jerome, as he advanced in life, would have developed every qualification requisite in a sovereign. Louis would have been distinguished in any rank or condition of life. My sister Eliza was endowed with masculine powers of mind; she must have proved herself a philosopher in her adverse fortune. Caroline possessed great talents and capacity. Pauline, perhaps the most beautiful woman of her age, has been and will continue to the end of her life, the most amiable creature in the world. As to my mother, she deserves all kinds of veneration. How seldom is so numerous a family entitled to so much praise. Add to this, that, setting aside the jarring of political opinions, we sincerely loved each other. For my part, I never ceased to cherish fraternal affection for them all. And I am convinced that in their hearts they felt the same sentiments toward me, and that in case of need, they would have given me every proof of it."

The proud old nobility, whom Napoleon had restored to France, and upon many of whom he had conferred their confiscated estates, manifested no gratitude toward their benefactor. They were sighting for the re-enthronement of the Bourbons, and for the return of the good old times, when all the offices of emolument and honor were reserved for them and for their children, and the people were but their hewers of wood and drawers of water. In the morning, as beggars, they would crowd the audience-chamber of the First Consul with their petitions. In the evening they disdained to honor his levees with their presence. They spoke contemptuously of Josephine, of her kindness and her desire to conciliate all parties. They condemned every thing that Napoleon did. He, however, paid no heed to their murmurings. He would not condescend even to punish them by neglect. In that most lofty pride which induced him to say that, in his administration he wished to imitate the elemency of God , he endeavored to consult for the interests of all, both the evil and the unthankful. His fame was to consist, not in revenging himself upon his enemies, but in aggrandizing France.

At this time Napoleon's establishment at the Tuileries rather resembled that of a very rich gentleman, than the court of a monarch. Junot, one of his aids, was married to Mademoiselle Permon, the young lady whose name will be remembered in connection with the anecdote of "Puss in Boots." Her mother was one of the most haughty of the ancient nobility, who affected to look upon Napoleon with contempt as not of royal blood. The evening after her marriage Madame Junot was to be presented to Josephine. After the Opera she drove to the Tuileries. It was near eleven o'clock. As Josephine had appointed the hour, she was expected. Eugene, hearing the wheels of the carriage, descended to the court-yard, presented his arm to Madame Junot, and they entered the large saloon together. It was a magnificent apartment, magnificently furnished. Two chandeliers, surrounded with gauze to soften the glare, shed a subdued and grateful light over the room. Josephine was seated before a tapestry-frame working upon embroidery. Near her sat Hortense, sylph-like in figure, and surpassingly gentle and graceful in her manners. Napoleon was standing near Josephine, with his hands clasped behind him, engaged in conversation with his wife and her lovely daughter. Upon the entrance of Madame Junot Josephine immediately arose, took her two hands, and, affectionately kissing her, said, "I have too long been Junot's friend, not to entertain the same sentiments for his wife; particularly for the one he has chosen."

"Oh, Josephine!" said Napoleon, "that is running on very fast. How do you know that this little pickle is worth loving. Well, Mademoiselle Loulou (you see that I do not forget the names of my old friends), have you not a word for me!" Saying this, he gently took her hand and drew her toward him.

The young bride was much embarrassed, and yet she struggled to retain her pride of birth. "General!" she replied, smiling, "it is not for me to speak first."

"Very well parried," said Napoleon, playfully, "the mother's spirit! And how is Madame Permon?"

"Very ill, general! For two years her health has caused us great uneasiness."

"Indeed," said Napoleon," so bad as that? I am sorry to hear it; very sorry. Make my regards to her. It is a wrong head, a proud spirit, but she has a generous heart and a noble soul. I hope that we shall often see you, Madame Junot. My intention is to draw around me a numerous family, consisting of my generals and their young wives. They will be of my wife and of Hortense, as their husbands are my friends. But you must not expect to meet here your acquaintances of the ancient nobility. I do not like them. They are my enemies, and prove it by defaming."

This was but the morning twilight of that imperial splendor which afterward dazzled the most powerful potentates of Europe. Hortense, who subsequently became the wife of Louis Bonaparte, and the mother of Louis Napoleon, who, at the moment of this present writing, is at the head of the government of France, was then seventeen years of age. "She was," Madame Junot, "fresh as a rose. Though her fair complexion was not relieved by much color, she had enough to produce that freshness and bloom which was her chief beauty. A profusion of light hair played in silken locks around her soft and penetrating blue eyes. The delicate roundness of her figure, slender as a palm-tree, was set off by the elegant carriage of her head. But that which formed the chief attraction of Hortense was the grace and suavity of her manners, which united the Creole nonchalance with the vivacity of France. She was gay, gentle, and amiable. She had wit, which, without the smallest ill-temper, had just malice enough to be amusing. A polished and well-conducted education had improved her natural talents. She drew excellently, sang harmoniously, and performed admirably in comedy. In 1800, she was a charming young girl. She afterward became one of the most amiable princesses in Europe. I have seen many, both in their own courts and in Paris, but I have never known one who had any pretensions to equal talents. She was beloved by every one. Her brother loved her tenderly. The First Consul looked upon her as his child."

Napoleon has been accused of an improper affection for Hortense. The world has been filled with the slander. Says Bourrienne, "Napoleon never cherished for her any feeling but a real paternal tenderness. He loved her after his marriage with her mother, as he would have loved his own child. At least for three years I was a witness to all their most private actions, and I declare I never saw any thing that could furnish the least ground for suspicion, nor the slightest trace of a culpable intimacy. This calumny must be classed among those which malice delights to take in the character of men who become celebrated, calumnies which are adopted lightly and without reflection. Napoleon is no more. Let his memory be accompanied only by that, be it good or bad, which really took place. Let not this reproach be made a charge against him by the impartial historian. I must say, in conclusion, on this delicate subject, that his principles were rigid in an extreme degree, and that any fault of the nature charged, neither entered his mind, nor was in accordance with his morals or his taste."

At St. Helena Napoleon was one day looking over a book containing an account of his amours. He smiled as he glanced his eye over the pages, saying, "I do not even know the names of most of the females who are mentioned here. This is all very foolish. Every body knows that had no time for such dissipation."

One beautiful evening, in the year 1815, the parish priest of San Pietro, a village a few miles distant from Sevilla, returned much fatigued to his little cottage, where he found his aged housekeeper, the Senora Margarita, watching for him. Notwithstanding that one is well accustomed to the sight of poverty in Spain, it was impossible to help being struck by the utter of destitution which appeared in the house of the good priest; the more so, as every imaginable contrivance had been restored to, to hide the nakedness of the walls, and the shabbiness of the furniture. Margarita had prepared for her master's super a rather small dish of olla-podriga , which consisted, to say the truth, of the remains of the dinner, seasoned and disguised with great skill, and with the addition of some sauce, and a name . As she placed the savory dish upon the table, the priest said: "We should thank God for this good supper, Margarita: this olla-podriga makes one's mouth water. My friend, you ought to be grateful for finding so good a supper at the house of your host!" At the word host, Margarita raised her eyes, and saw a stranger, who had followed her mater. Her countenance changed, and she looked annoyed. .... She glanced indignantly first at the unknown, and then at the priest, who, looking down, said in a low voice, and with the timidity of a child: "What is enough for two, is always enough for three; and surely you would not wish that I should allow a Christian to die of hunger? He has not tasted food for two days."

"A Christian! He is more like a brigand!" and Margarita let the room, murmuring loudly enough to be heard.

Meanwhile, the unwelcome guest had remained standing at the door. He was a man of great height, half-dressed in rags and covered with mud; while his black hair, piercing eyes, and carbine, gave him an appearance which, though hardly prepossessing, was certainly interesting. "Must I go?" said he.

The priest replied with an emphatic gesture: "Those whom I bring under my roof are never driven forth, and are never unwelcome. Put down your carbine. Let us say grace, and go to table."

"I never leave my carbine, for, as the Castilian proverb says, "Two friends are one.' My carbine is my best friend; and I always keep it beside me. Although you allow me to come into your house, and do not oblige me to leave until I wish to do so, there are others who would think nothing of hauling me out, and perhaps, with me feet foremost. Come--to your good health, mine host, and let us to supper."

The priest possessed an extremely good appetite, but the voracity of the stranger soon obliged him to give up, for not contented with eating, or rather devouring, nearly the whole of the olla-podriga, the guest finished a large loaf of bread, without leaving a crumb. While he ate, he kept continually looking round with an expression of inquietude: he started at the slightest sound; and once, when a violent gust of wind made the door bang, he sprang to his feet, and seized his carbine, with an air which showed that, if necessary, he would sell his life dearly. Discovering the cause of the alarm, he reseated himself at table, and finished his repast.

"Now," said he, "I have one thing more to ask. I have been wounded, and for eight days my wound has not been dressed. Give me a few old rags, and you shall be no longer burdened with my presence."

"I am in no haste for you to go," replied the priest, whose quest, notwithstanding his constant watchfulness, had conversed very entertainingly. "I know something of surgery, and will dress your wound."

So saying, he took from a cupboard a case containing every thing necessary, and proceeded to do as he had said. The stranger had bled profusely, a ball having passed through his thigh; and to have traveled in this condition, and while suffering, too, from want of food, showed a strength, which seemed hardly human.

"You can not possibly continue your journey to-day," said the host. "You must pass the night here. A little rest will get up your strength, diminish the inflammation of your wound, and--"

"I must go to--day, and immediately," interrupted the stranger. "There are some who wait for me," he added with a sigh--"and there are some, too,who follow me." And the momentary look of softness passed from his features between the clauses of the sentence, and gave place to an expression almost of ferocity. "Now, is it finished? That is well. See, I can walk as firmly as though I had never been wounded. Give me some bread: pay yourself for your hospitality with this piece of gold, and adieu."

The priest put back the gold with displeasure. "I am not an innkeeper, said he; "and I do not sell my hospitality."

"As you will, but pardon me; and now farewell, my kind host."

So saying he took the bread, which Margarita, at her master's command, very unwillingly gave him, and soon his tall figure disappeared among the thick foliage of a wood which surrounded the house, or rather the cabin. An hour had scarcely passed, when musket-shots were heard close by, and the unknown reappeared, deadly pale, and bleeding from a deep wound near the heart.

"Take these," said he, giving pieces of gold to his late host; "they are for my children--near the stream--in the valley."

[missing pages]

deadly agency, which it had power to exert. Even the roadway leading up and down the mountain is not always safe, it would seem, from these dangerous intruders. It is rocky and solitary, and is bordered every where with gloomy ravines and chasms, all filled with dense and entangled thickets, in which, and in the cavernous rocks of which the strata of the mountain are composed, wild beast and noxious animals of every kind find a secure retreat. The monks relate that not many years ago a servant of the convent, who had been sent down the mountain to Haifa, to accompany a traveler, was attacked and seized by a panther on his return. The panther, however, instead of putting his victim immediately to death, began to play with him as a cat plays with a mouse which she has succeeded in making her prey-holding him gently with her claws, for a time, and then, after drawing back a little, darting upon him again, as if to repeat and renew the pleasure of capturing such a prize. This was continued so long, that the cries of the terrified captive brought to the spot some persons that chanced to be near, when the panther was terrified in her turn, and fled into the forests; and then the man was rescued from his horrible situation unharmed.

For these and similar reasons, travelers who ascend to the convent of Mt. Carmel, enjoy but little liberty there, but most confine their explorations in most cases to the buildings of the monks, and to some of the nearest caves of the ancient recluses. Still the spot is rendered so attractive by the salubrity of the air, the intrinsic beauty of the situation, the magnificence of the prospect, and the kind and attentive demeanor of the monks, that some visitors have recommended it as a place of permanent resort for those who leave their homes in the West in pursuit of health, or in search of retirement and repose. The rule that requires those who have been guests of the convent more than two weeks to give place to others more recently arrived, proves in facto be no serious difficulty. Some kind of an arrangement can in such cases always, be made, though it is seldom that any occasion arises that requires it. The quarters, too, though plain and simple are comfortable and neat, and although the visitor is somewhat restricted, from causes that have already been named, in respect to explorations of the mountain itself, there are many excursions that can be made in the country below, of a very attractive character. He can visit Haifa, he can ride or walk along the beach to Acre; he can go to Nazareth, or journey down the coast, passing round the western declivity of the mountain. In these and similar rambles he will find scenes of continual novelty to attract him, and be surrounded every where with the forms and usages of Oriental life.

The traveler who comes to Mt. Carmel by the way .... of Nazareth and the plain of Esdraelon, in going away from it generally passes round the western declivity of the mountain, and thence proceeds to the south, by the way of the sea. On reaching the foot of the descent, where the mountain mule-path comes out into the main road, as shown upon the map near the commencement of this article, he turns shorts to the left, and goes on round the base of the promontory, with the lofty declivities of the mountain on one hand, and a mass of dense forests on the other, lying between the road and the shore. As he passes on, the road, picturesque and romantic from the beginning becomes gradually wild, solitary, and desolate. It leads him sometimes through tangled thickets, sometimes under shelving rocks, and sometimes it brings him out unexpectedly to the shore of the sea, where he sees the surf rolling in upon the beach at his feet, and far over the water the setting sun going down to his rest beneath the western horizon. At length the twilight gradually disappears, and as the shades of the evening come on, lights glimmer in the solitary villages that he passes on his way; but there is no welcome for him in their beaming. At length when he deems it time to bring his day's journey to an end, he pitches his tent by the wayside in some unfrequented spot, and before he retires to rest for the night, comes out to take one more view of the dark and sombre mountain which he is about to leave forever. He stands at the door of his tent, and gazes at it long and earnestly, before he bids it farewell, equally impressed with the sublime magnificence of its situation and form, and with the solemn grandeur of its history.

France was now at peace with all the world. It was universally admitted that Napoleon was the great pacificator. He was the idol of France. The masses of the people in Europe, every where regarded him as their advocate and friend, the enemy of aristocratic usurpation, and the great champion of equality. The people of France no longer demanded liberty . Weary years of woe had taught them gladly to relinquish the boon. They only desired a ruler who would take care of them, govern them, protect them from the power of allied despotism, and give them equal rights. Though Napoleon had now but the title of First

Consul, and France was nominally a republic, he was in reality the most powerful monarch in Europe. His throne was established in the hearts of nearly forty millions of people. His word was law.

It will be remembered that Josephine contemplated the extraordinary grandeur to which her husband had attained, with intense solicitude. She saw that more that than ordinary regal power had passed into his hands, and she was not a stranger to the intense desire which animated his heart to have an heir to whom to transmit his name and his glory. She knew that many were intimating to him that an heir was essential to the repose of France. She was fully informed that divorce had been urged upon him as one of the stern necessities of state. One day, when Napoleon was busy in his cabinet, Josephine entered softly, by a side door, and seating herself affectionately upon his knee, and passing her hand gently through his hair, said to him, with a burst of tenderness, "I entreat you, my friend, do not make yourself king. It is Lucien who urges you to it. Do not listen to him." Napoleon smiled upon her kindly, and said, "Why, my poor Josephine, you are mad. You must not listen to these fables which the old dowagers, tell you. But you interrupt me now; I am very busy; leave me alone."

It is recorded that Lucien ventured to suggest to Josephine that a law higher than the law of ordinary morality required that she must become a mother, even were it necessary, for the attainment of that end, that she should violate her nuptial vows. Brutalizing and vulgar infidelity had obliterated in France, nearly all the sacredness of domestic ties. Josephine, instinctively virtuous, and revering the religion of her childhood, which her husband had reinstated, bursting into tears, indignantly exclaimed, "This is dreadful. Wretched should I be were any one to suppose me capable of listening, without horror, to your infamous proposal. Your ideas are poisonous; your language horrible." "Well, then, madame," responded Lucien, "all that I can say is, that from my heart I pity you."

Josephine was at times almost delirious in apprehension of the awful calamity which threatened her. She knew the intensity of her husband's love.

She also knew the boundlessness of his ambition. She could not be blind to the apparent importance, as a matter of state policy that Napoleon should possess an heir. She also was fully aware that throughout France marriage had long been regarded but as a partnership of convenience, to be formed and sundered almost at pleasure. "Marriage," said Madame de Stael, has become but the sacrament of adultery." The nation, under the influence of these views, would condemn her for selfishly refusing assent to an arrangement apparently essential to the repose of France and of Europe Never was a woman placed in a situation of more terrible trial. Never was an ambitious man exposed to a more fiery temptation. Laying aside the authority of Christianity, and contemplating the subject in the light of mere expediency, it seemed a plain duty for Napoleon and Josephine to separate. But gloriously does it illustrate the immutable truth of God's word, that even in such an exigence as this, the path which the Bible pointed out was the only path of safety and of peace. "In separating myself from Josephine," said Napoleon afterward, "and in marrying Maria Louisa, I placed my foot upon an abyss which was covered with flowers."

Josephine's daughter, Hortense, beautiful, brilliant, and amiable, then but eighteen years of age, was strongly attached to Duroc, one of Napoleon's aids, a very fashionable and handsome man. Josephine, however, had conceived the idea of marrying Hortense to Louis Bonaparte, Napoleon's younger brother. She said, one day, to Bourrienne, "My two brothers-in-law are my determined enemies. You see all their intrigues. You know how much uneasiness they have caused me. This projected marriage with Duroc, leaves me without any support. Duroc, independent of Bonaparte's friendship, is nothing. He has neither fortune, rank, nor even reputation. He can afford me no protection against the enmity of the brothers. I must have some more certain reliance for the future. My husband loves Louis very much. If I can succeed in uniting my daughter to him, he will prove a strong counterpoise to the calumnies and persecutions of my brothers-in-law." These remarks were reported to Napoleon. He replied, "Josephine labors in vain. Duroc and Hortense love each other, and they shall be married. I am attached to Duroc. He is well born. I have given Caroline to Murat, and Pauline to Le Clerc. I can as well give

Hortense to Duroc. He is brave. He is as good as the others. He is general of division. Besides, I have other views for Louis."

In the palace the heart may throb with the same joys and griefs as in the cottage. In anticipation of the projected marriage Duroc was sent on a special mission to compliment the Emperor Alexander on his accession to the throne. Duroc wrote often to Hortense while absent. When the private secretary whispered in her ears, in the midst of the brilliant throng of the Tuileries, "I have a letter," she would immediately retire to her apartment. Upon her return her friends could see that her eyes were moistened with the tears of affection and joy. Josephine cherished the hope that could she succeed in uniting Hortense with Louis Bonaparte, should Hortense give birth to a son, Napoleon would regard him as his heir. The child would bear the name of Bonaparte; the blood of the Bonapartes would circulate in his veins; and he would be the offspring of Hortense, whom Napoleon regarded as his own daughter, and whom he loved with the strongest parental affection. Thus the terrible divorce might be averted. Urged by motives so powerful, Josephine left no means untried to accomplish her purpose.

Louis Bonaparte was a studious, pensive, imaginative man, of great moral worth, though possessing but little force of character. He had been bitterly disappointed in his affections, and was weary of the world. When but nineteen years of age he had formed a very strong attachment for a young lady whom he had met in Paris. She was the daughter of an emigrant noble, and his whole being because absorbed in the passion of love. Napoleon, then in the midst of those victories which paved his way to the throne of France, was apprehensive that the alliance of his brother with one of the old royalist families, might endanger his own ambitious projects. He therefore sent him away on a military commission, and secured, by his powerful instrumentality, the marriage of the young lady to another person. The disappointment preyed deeply upon the heart of the sensitive young man. All ambition died within him. He loved solitude, and studiously avoided the cares and pomp of state. Napoleon, not having been aware of the extreme strength of his brother's attachment, when he saw the wound which he had inflicted upon him, endeavored to make all the amends in his power. Hortense was beautiful, full of grace and vivacity. At last Napoleon fell in with the views of Josephine, and resolved, having united the two, to recompense his brother, as far as possible, by lavishing great favors upon them.

It was long before Louis would listen to the proposition of his marriage with Hortense. His affections still clung to the lost object of his idolatry, and he could not, without pain, think of union with another. Indeed a more uncongenial alliance could hardly have been imagined. In no one thing were their tastes similar. But who could resist the combined tact of Josephine and power of Napoleon. All obstacles were swept away, and the maiden, loving the hilarity of life, and its gayest scenes of festivity and splendor, was reluctantly led to the silent, pensive scholar, who as reluctantly received her as his bride. Hortense had become in some degree reconciled to the match, as her powerful father promised to place them in high positions of wealth and rank. Louis resigned himself to his lot, feeling the earth had no further joy in store for him. A magnificent fete was given in honor of this marriage, at which all the splendors of the ancient royalty were revived. Louis Napoleon Bonaparte, who, as President of the French Republic, succeeded Louis Philippe, the King of the French, was the only child of this marriage who survived his parents.

Napoleon had organized in the heart of Italy a republic containing about five millions of inhabitants. This republic could by no means maintain itself against the monarchies of Europe, unaided by France. Napoleon, surrounded by hostile kings, deemed it essential to the safety of France, to secure in Italy a nation of congenial sympathies and interests, with whom he could form the alliance of cordial friendship. The Italians, all inexperienced in self-government, regarding Napoleon as their benefactor and their sole supporter, looked to him for a constitution. Three of the most influential men of the Cisalpine Republic, were sent as delegates to Paris, to consult with the First Consul upon the organization of their government. Under the direction of Napoleon a constitution was drafted, which, considering the character of the Italian people, and the hostile monarchicals influences which surrounded them, was most highly liberal. A President was Vice-President were to be chosen for ten years. There was to be a Senate of eight members and a House of Representatives of seventy-five members. There were all to be selected from a body composed of 300 landed proprietors, 200 of the clergy and prominent literary men. Thus all the important interests of the state were represented.

In Italy, as in all the other countries of Europe at that time, there were three prominent parties. The Loyalists sought the restoration of monarchy and the exclusive privileges of kings and nobles. The Moderate Republicans wished to establish a firm government, which would enforce order and confer upon all equal rights. The Jacobins wished to break down all distinctions, divide property, and to govern by the blind energies of the mob. Italy had long been held in subjection by the spiritual terrors of the priests and by the bayonets of the Austrians. Ages of bondage had enervated the people and there were no Italian statesmen capable of taking the helm of government in such a turbulent sea of troubles. Napoleon resolved to have himself proposed as President, and then reserving to himself the supreme direction, to delegate the details of affairs to distinguished Italians, until they should, in some degree, be trained to duties so new to them. Says Theirs. "This plan was not, on his part, the inspiration of ambition, but rather of great good sense. His views on this occasion were unquestionably both pure and exalted." But nothing can more strikingly show the almost miraculous energies of Napoleon's mind, and his perfect self-reliance, than the readiness with which, in addition to the cares of the Empire of France, he assumed the responsibility of organizing and developing another nation of five millions of inhabitants. This was in 1802. Napoleon was then but thirty-three years of age.

To have surrendered those Italians, who had rallied around the armies of France in their hour of need, again to Austrian domination, would have been an act of treachery. To have abandoned them, in their inexperience, to the Jacobin mob on the one hand, and to royalist intrigues on the other, would have insured the ruin of the Republic. But by leaving the details of government to be administered by Italians, and at the same time sustaining the constitution by his own powerful hand, there was a probability that the republic might attain prosperity and independence. As the press of business rendered it extremely difficult for Napoleon to leave France, a plan was formed for a vast congress of the Italians, to be assembled in Lyons, about half way between Paris and Milan, for the imposing adoption of the republican constitution. Four hundred and fifty-two deputies were elected to cross the frozen Alps, in the month of December. The extraodinary watchfulness and foresight of the First Consul, had prepared every comfort for them on the way. In Lyons sumptuous preparations were made for their entertainment. Magnificent halls were decorated in the highest style of earthly splendor for the solemnities of the occasion. The army of Egypt, which had recently landed, bronzed by an African sun was gorgeously attired to add to the magnificence of the spectacle. The Lyonese youth, exultant with pride, were formed into an imposing body of cavalry. On the 11th of January, 1802, Napoleon, accompanied by Josephine, arrived in Lyons. The whole population of the adjoining country had assembled along the road, anxiously watching for his passage. At night immense fires illumined his path, blazing upon every hill side and in every valley. One continuous shout of "Live Bonaparte," rolled along with the carriage from Paris to Lyons. It was late in the evening when Napoleon arrived in Lyons. The brilliant city flamed with the splendor of noon-day. The carriage of the First Consul passed under a triumphal arch, surmounted by a sleeping lion, the emblem of France, and Napoleon took up his residence in the Hotel deVille, which, in most princely sumptuousness had been decorated for his reception. The Italians adored Napoleon. They felt personally ennobled by his renown, for they considered him their countryman. The Italian language was his native tongue, and he spoke it with the most perfect fluency and elegance. The moment that the name of Napoleon was suggested to the deputies as President of the Republic, it was received with shouts of enthusiastic acclamation. A deputation was immediately send to the First Consul to express the unanimous and cordial wish of the convention that he would accept the office. While these things were transpiring, Napoleon, ever intensely occupied, was inspecting his veteran soldiers of Italy and of Egypt, in a public review. The elements seemed to conspire to invest the occasion with splendor. The day was cloudless, the sun brilliant, the sky serene, the air invigorating. All the inhabitants of Lyons and the populace of the adjacent country thronged the streets. No pen can describe the transports with which the hero was received, as he rode along the lines of these veterans, whom he had so often led to victory. The soldiers shouted in a frenzy of enthusiasm. Old men, and young men, and boys caught the shout and it reverberated along the streets in one continuous roar. Matrons and maidens, waving banners and handkerchiefs, wept in excess of emotion. Bouquets of flowers were showered from the windows, to carpet his path, and every conceivable demonstration was made of the most enthusiastic love. Napoleon himself was deeply moved by the scene. Some of the old grenadiers, whom he recognized, he called out of the ranks, kindly talked with them, inquiring respecting their wounds and their wants. He addressed several of the officers, whom he had seen in many encounters, shook hands with them, and a delirium of excitement pervaded all minds Upon his return to the Hotel deVille, he met the deputation of the convention. They presented him the address, urging upon him the acceptance of the Presidency of the Cisalpine Republic. Napoleon received the address, intimated his acceptance, and promised, on the following day, to meet the convention.

The next morning dawned brightly upon the city. A large church, embellished with richest drapery, was prepared for the solemnities of the occasion. Napoleon entered the church, took his seat upon an elevated platform, surrounded by his family, the French ministers, and a large number of distinguished generals and statesmen. He addressed the assembly in the Italian language, with as much ease of manner, elegance of expression, and fluency of utterance as if his whole life had been devoted to the cultivation of the powers of oratory. He announced his acceptance of the dignity with which they would invest him and uttered his views respecting the measures which he adopted to secure the prosperity of the Italian Republic , as the new state was henceforth to be called. Repeated bursts of applause interrupted his address, and at its close one continuous shout of acclamation testified the assent and the delight of the assembled multitude. Napoleon remained at Lyons twenty days, occupied, apparently every moment, with the vast affairs which then engrossed his attention. And yet he found time to write daily to Paris, urging forward the majestic enterprises of the new government in France. The following brief extracts from this free and confidential correspondence, afford an interesting glimpse of the motives which actuated Napoleon at this time, and of the great objects of his ambition.

"I am proceeding slowly in my operations. I pass the whole of my mornings in giving audience to the deputations of the neighboring departments. The improvement in the happiness of France is obvious. During the past two years the population of Lyons has increased more than 20,000 souls. All the manufacturers tell me that their works are in a state of high activity. All minds seem to be full of energy, not that energy which overturns empires, but that which re-establishes them, and conducts them to prosperity and riches."

"I beg of you particularly to see that the unruly members, whom we have in the constituted authorities, are every one of them removed. The wish of the nation is, that the government shall not be obstructed in its endeavors to act for the public good, and that the head of Medusa shall no longer show itself, either in our tribunes or in our assemblies. The conduct of Sieyes, on this occasion, completely proves that having contributed to the destruction of all the constitutions since '91, he wishes now to try his hand against the present. He ought to burn a wax candle to Our Lady, for having got out of the scrape so fortunately and in so unexpected a manner. But the older I grow, the more I perceive that each man must fulfill his destiny. I recommend you to ascertain whether the provisions for St. Domingo have actually been sent off. I take it for granted that you have taken proper measures for demolishing the Chatelet. If the Minister of Marine should stand in need of the frigates of the King of Naples, he may make use of them. General Jourdan gives me a satisfactory account of the state of Piedmont."

"I wish that citizen Royer be sent to the 16th military division, to examine into the accounts of the paymaster. I also wish some individual, like citizen Royer, to perform the same duty for the 13th and 14th divisions. It is complained that the receivers keep the money as long as they can, and that the paymasters postpone payment as long as possible. The paymasters and the receivers are the greatest nuisance in the state."

"Yesterday I visited several factories. I was pleased with the industry and the severe economy which pervaded these establishments. Should the wintry weather continue severe, I do not think that the $25,000 a month, which the Minister of the Interior grants for the purposes of charity, will be sufficient. It will be necessary to add five thousand dollars for the distribution of wood, and also to light fires in the churches and other large buildings to give warmth to a great number of people."

Napoleon arrived in Paris on the 31st of January. In the mean time, there had been a new election of members of the Tribunate and of the Legislative body. All those who had manifested any opposition to the measures of Napoleon, in the re-establishment of Christianity, and in the adoption of the new civil code, were left out, and their places supplied by those who approved of the measures of the First Consul. Napoleon could now act unembarrassed. In every quarter there was submission. All the officers of the state, immediately upon his return, sought an audience, and in that pomp of language which his majestic deeds and character inspired, presented to him their congratulations. He was already a sovereign, in possession of regal power, such as no other monarch in Europe enjoyed. Upon one object all the energies of his mighty mind were concentrated. France was his estate, his diadem, his all. The glory of France was his glory, the happiness of France his happiness, the riches of France his wealth. Never did a father with more untiring self-denial and toil labor for his family, than did Napoleon through days of Herculean exertion and nights of sleeplessness devote every energy of body and soul to the greatness of France. He loved not ease, he loved not personal indulgence, he loved not sensual gratification. The elevation of France to prosperity, wealth, and power, was a limitless ambition. The almost supernatural success which had thus far attended his exertions, did but magnify his desires and stimulate his hopes. He had no wish to elevate France upon the ruins of other nations. But he wished to make France the pattern of all excellence, the illustrious leader at the head of all nations, guiding them to intelligence, to opulence, and to happiness. Such, at this time, was the towering ambition of Napoleon, the most noble and comprehensive which was ever embraced by the conception of man. Of course, such ambition was not consistent with the equality of other nations for he determined that France should be the first. But he manifested no disposition to destroy the prosperity of others; he only wished to give such an impulse to humanity in France, by the culture of mind, by purity of morals, by domestic industry, by foreign commerce, by great national works, as to place France in the advance upon the race course of greatness. In this race France had but one antagonist--England. France had nearly forty millions of inhabitants. The island of Great Britain contained but about fifteen millions. But England, with her colonies, girdled the globe, and, with her fleets, commanded all seas. "France," said Napoleon, "must also have her colonies and her fleets." "If we permit that," the statesman of England rejoined, "we may become a secondary power, and may thus be at the mercy of France." It was undeniably so. Shall history be blind to such fatality as this? Is man, in the hour of triumphant ambition, so moderate, that we can be willing that he should attain power which places us at his mercy? England was omnipotent upon the seas. She became arrogant, and abused that power, and made herself offensive to all nations. Napoleon developed no special meekness of character to indicate that he would be, in the pride of strength which no nation could resist, more moderate and conciliating. Candor can not censure England for being unwilling to yield her high position to surrender her supremacy on the seas--to become a secondary power--to allow France to become her master. And who can censure France for seeking the establishment of colonies, the extension of commerce, friendly alliance with other nations, and the creation of fleets to protect her from aggression upon the ocean, as well as upon the land? Napoleon himself, with that wonderful magnanimity which ever characterized him, though at times exasperated by the hostility which he now encountered yet often spoke in terms of respect of the influences which animated his foes. It is to be regretted that his antagonists so seldom reciprocated this magnanimity. There was here, most certainly, a right and a wrong. But it is not easy for man accurately to adjust the balance. God alone can award the issue. The mind is saddened as it wanders amid the labyrinths of conscientiousness and of passion, of pure motives and impure ambition. This is, indeed, a fallen world. The drama of nations is a tragedy. Melancholy is the lot of man.

England daily witnessed, with increasing alarm, the rapid and enormous strides which France was making. The energy of the First Consul seemed superhuman. His acts indicated the most profound sagacity, the most far-reaching foresight. To-day the news reaches London that Napoleon has been elected President of the Italian Republic. Thus in an hour five millions of people are added to his empire! To-morrow it is announced that he is establishing a colony at Elba, that a vast expedition is sailing for St. Domingo, to re-organize the colony there. England is bewildered. Again it is proclaimed that Napoleon has purchased Louisiana of Spain, and is preparing to fill the fertile valley of the Mississippi with colonists. In the mean time, all France is in a state of activity. Factories, roads, bridges, canals, fortifications are every where springing into existence. The sound of the ship hammer reverberates in all the harbors of France, and every month witnesses the increase of the French fleet. The mass of the English people contemplate with admiration this development of energy. The statesmen of England contemplate it with dread.

For some months, Napoleon, in the midst of all his other cares, had been maturing a vast system of public instruction for the youth of France. He drew up, with his own hand, the plan for their schools, and proposed the course of study. It is a little singular that, with his strong scientific predilections, he should have assigned the first rank to classical studies. Perhaps this is to be accounted for from his profound admiration of the heroes of antiquity. His own mind was most thoroughly stored with all the treasures of Greek and Roman story. All these schools were formed upon a military model, for situated as France was, in the midst of monarchies, at heart hostile, he deemed it necessary that the nation should be universally trained to bear arms. Religious instruction was to be communicated in all these schools by chaplains, military instruction by old officers who had left the army, and classical and scientific instruction by the most learned men Europe could furnish. The First Consul also devoted special attention to female schools. "France needs nothing so much to promote her regeneration," said he, "as good mothers." To attract the youth of France to these schools, one millions of dollars was appropriated for over six thousand gratuitous exhibitions for the pupils. Ten schools of law were established, nine schools of medicine, and an institution for the mechanical arts, called the "School of Bridges and Roads," the first model of those schools of art which continue in France until the present day, and which are deemed invaluable. There were no exclusive privileges in these institutions. A system of perfect equality pervaded them. The pupils of all classes were placed upon a level, with an unobstructed arena before them. "This is only a commencement," said Napoleon, "by-and-by we shall do more and better."

Another project which Napoleon now introduced was vehemently opposed-- the establishment of the Legion of Honor. One of the leading principles of the revolution was the entire overthrow of all titles of distinction. Every man, high or low, was to be addressed simply as Citizen . Napoleon wished to introduce a system of rewards which should stimulate to heroic deeds, and which should ennoble those who had deserved well of humanity. Innumerable foreigners of distinction had thronged France since the peace. He had observed with what eagerness the populace had followed these foreigners, gazing with delight upon their gay decorations The court-yard of the Tuileries was ever crowded when these illustrious strangers arrived and departed. Napoleon, in his council, where he was always eloquent and powerful, thus urged his views:

"Look at these vanities, which genius pretends so much to disdain. The populace is not of that opinion. It loves these many-colored ribbons, as it loves religious pomp. The democrat philosopher calls it vanity. Vanity let it be. But that vanity is a weakness common to the whole human race, and great virtues may be made to spring from it. With these so much despised baubles heroes are made. There must be worship for the religious sentiment. There must be visible distinctions for the noble sentiment of glory. Nations should not strive to be singular any more than individuals. The affectation of acting differently from the rest of the world, is an affectation which is reproved by all persons of sense and modesty. Ribbons are in use in all countries. Let them be in use in France. It will be one more friendly relation established with Europe. Our neighbors give them only to the man of noble birth. I will give them to the man of merit--to the one who shall have served best in the army or in the state, or who shall have produced the finest works."

It was objected that the institution of the Legion of Honor was a return to the aristocracy which the revolution had abolished. "What is there aristocratic," Napoleon exclaimed, "in a distinction purely personal, and merely for life, bestowed on the man who has displayed merit, whether evil or military-- bestowed on him alone, bestowed for his life only, and not passing to his children. Such a distinction is the reverse of aristocratic. It is the essence of aristocracy that its titles are transmitted from the man who has earned them, to the son who possesses no merit. The ancient regime, so battered by the ram revolution, is more entire than is believed. All the emigrants hold each other by the hand. The Vendeeans are secretly enrolled. The priests, at heart, are not very friendly to us. With the words 'legitimate king,' thousands might be roused to arms. It is needful that the men who have taken part in the revolution should have a bond of union, and cease to depend on the first accident which might strike one single head. For ten years we have only been making ruins. We must now found an edifice. Depend upon it, the struggle is not over with Europe. Be assured that struggle will begin again"

It was then urged by some, that the Legion of Honor should be confined entirely to military merit. "By no means," said Napoleon, "Rewards are not to be conferred upon soldiers alone. All sorts of merit are brothers. The courage of the President of the Convention, resisting the populace, should compared with the courage of Kleber, mounting to the assault of Acre. It is right that civil virtues should have their reward, as well as military virtues. Those who oppose this course, reason like barbarians. It is the religion of brute force they commend to us. Intelligence has its rights before those of force. Force, without intelligence, is nothing. In barbarous ages, the man of stoutest sinews was the chieftain. Now the general is the most intelligent of the brave. At Cairo, the Egyptians could not comprehend how it was that Kleber, with his majestic form, was not commander-in-chief. When Mourad Bey had carefully observed our tactics, he could comprehend how it was that I, and no other, ought to be the general of an army so conducted. You reason like the Egyptians, when you attempt to confine rewards to military valor. The soldiers reason better than you. Go to their bivouacs; listen to them. Do you imagine that it is the tallest of their officers, and the most imposing by his stature, for whom they feel the highest regard! Do you imagine even that the bravest stands first in their esteem. No doubt they would despise the man whose courage they suspected; but they rank above the merely brave man him who they consider the most intelligent. As for myself, do you suppose that it is solely because I am reputed a great general that I rule France! No! It is because the qualities of a statesman and a magistrate are attributed to me. France will never tolerate the government of the sword. Those who think so are strangely mistaken. It would require an abject servitude of fifty years before that could be the case. France is too noble, too intelligent a country to submit to material power. Let us honor intelligence, virtue, the civil qualities; in short let us bestow upon them, in all profession, the like reward."

The true spirit of republicanism is certainly equality of rights, not of attainments and honors; the abolition of hereditary distinctions and privileges, not of those which are founded upon merit. The badge of the Legion of Honor was to be conferred upon all who, by genius, self-denial, and toil, had won renown. The prizes were open to the humblest peasant in the land. Still the popular hostility to any institution which bore a resemblance to the aristocracy of the ancient nobility was so strong, that though a majority voted in favor of the measure, there was a strong opposition. Napoleon was surprised. He said to Bourrienne: "You are right. Prejudices are still against me. I ought to have waited. There was no occasion for haste in bringing it forward. But the thing is done; and you will soon find that the taste for these distinctions is not yet gone by. It is a taste which belongs to the nature of man. You will see that extraordinary results will arise from it."

The order was consist of six thousand members. It was constituted in four ranks: grand officers, commanders, officers, and private legionaries. The badge was simply a red ribbon, in the button-hole. To the first rank, there was allotted an annual salary of $1000; to the second $400; to the third, $200; to the fourth, $50. The private soldier, the retired scholar, and the skillful artist were thus decorated with the same badge of distinction which figured upon the breast of generals, nobles and monarchs. That this institution was peculiarly adapted to the state of France, is evident from the fact, that it has survived all the revolutions of subsequent years. "Though of such recent origin," says

Theirs, "it is already consecrated as if it had passed through centuries; to such a degree has it become the recompense of heroism, of knowledge, of merit of every kind--so much have its honors been coveted by the grandees and the princes of Europe the most proud of their origin."

The popularity of Napoleon was now unbounded. A very general and earnest disposition was expressed to confer upon the First Consul a magnificent testimonial of the national gratitude--a testimonial worthy of the illustrious man who was to receive it, and of the powerful nation by which it was to be bestowed. The President of the Tribunal thus addressed that body: "Among all nations public honors have been decreed to men who, by splendid actions, have honored their country, and saved it from great dangers. What man ever had stronger claims to the national gratitude than General Bonaparte? His valor and genius have saved the French people from the excesses of anarchy, and from the miseries of war; and France is too great, too magnanimous to leave such benefits without reward."

A deputation was immediately chosen to confer with Napoleon upon the subject of the tribute of gratitude and affection which he should receive. Surrounded by his colleagues and the principal officers of the state, he received them the next day in the Tuileries. With seriousness and modesty he listened to the high eulogium upon his achievements which was pronounced, and then replaced. "I receive with sincere gratitude the wish to expressed by the Tribunate. I desire no other glory than having completely performed the task impose upon me. I aspire to no other reward than the affection of my fellow-citizens. I shall be happy if they are thoroughly convinced, that the evils which they may experience, will always be to me the severest of misfortunes; that life is dear to me solely for the services which I am to render to my country; that death itself will have no bitterness for me, if my last looks can see the happiness of the republic as firmly secured as is its glory." ....

But how was Napoleon to be rewarded! That was the great difficult question. Was wealth to be conferred upon him! For wealth he cared nothing Millions had been at his disposal, and he had emptied them all into the treasury of

France. Ease, luxury, self-indulgence had no charms for him. Were monuments to be reared to his honor, titles to be lavished upon his name? Napoleon regarded these but means for the accomplishment of ends. In themselves they were nothing. The one only thing which he desired was power, power to work out vast results for others, and thus to secure for himself renown, which should be pure and imperishable. But how could the power of Napoleon be increased! He was already almost absolute. Whatever he willed, he accomplished. Senators, legislators, and tribunes all co-operated in giving energy to his plans. It will be remembered, that Napoleon was elected First Consul for a period of ten years. It seemed that there was absolutely nothing which could be done, gratifying to the First Consul, but to prolong the term of his Consulship, by either adding to it another period of ten years, or by continuing it during his life. "What does he wish?" was the universal inquiry. Every possible means were tried, but in vain, to obtain a single word from his lips, significant of his desires. One of the senators went to Cambaceres, and said, "What would be gratifying to General Bonaparte? Does he wish to be king? Only let him say so, and we are all ready to vote for the re-establishment of royalty. Most willingly will we do it for him, for he is worthy of that station." But the First Consul shut himself up in impenetrable reserve. Even his most intimate friends could catch no glimpse of his secret wishes. At last the question was plainly and earnestly put to him. With great apparent humility, he replied: "I have not fixed my mind upon any thing. Any testimony of the public confidence will be sufficient for me, and will fill me with satisfaction." The question was then discussed whether to add ten years to his Consulship, or to make him First Consul for life. Cambaceres knew well the boundless ambition of Napoleon, and was fully conscious, that any limited period of power would not be in accordance with his plans. He ventured to say to him "You are wrong not to explain yourself. Your enemies, for notwithstanding your services, you have some left even in the Senate, will abuse your reserve." Napoleon calmly replied: "Let them alone. The majority of the Senate is always ready to do more than it is asked. They will go further than you imagine."

On the evening of the 8th of May, 1802, the resolution was adopted, of prolonging the powers of the First Consul for ten years . Napoleon was probably surprised and disappointed. He however, decided to return a grateful answer, and to say that from the Senate, but from the suffrages of the people alone could he accept a prolongation of that power to which their voices had elevated him. The following answer was transmitted to the Senate, the next morning:

"The honorable proof of your esteem, given in your deliberation of the 8th, will remain forever engraven on my heart. In the three years which have just elapsed fortune has smiled upon the republic. But fortune is fickle. How many men whom she has loaded with favors, have lived a few years too long. The interest of my glory and that of my happiness, would seem to have marked the term of my public life, at the moment when the peace of the world is proclaimed. But the glory and the happiness of the citizen ought to be silent, when the interest of the state, and the public partiality, call him. You judge that I owe a new sacrifice to the people. I will make it, if the wishes of the people command what your suffrage authorizes."

Napoleon immediately left Paris for his country-seat at Malmaison. This beautiful chateau was about ten miles from the metropolis. Josephine had purchased the peaceful, rural retreat at Napoleon's request during his first Italian campaign. Subsequently, large sums had been expended in enlarging and improving the grounds; and it was ever the favorite the grounds; and it was ever the favorite residence of both Josephine and Napoleon. Cambacres called an extraordinary meeting of the Council of State. After much deliberation, it was resolved, by an immense majority, that the following preposition should be submitted to the people: "Shall Napoleon Bonaparte be the First Consul for life? It was then resolved to submit a second question: " Shall the First Consul have the power of appointing his successor? This was indeed re-establishing monarchy, under a republican name.

Cambaceres immediately repaired to Malmaison, to submit these resolutions to Napoleon. To the amazement of all, he immediately and firmly rejected the second question. Energetically, he said "Whom would you have me appoint my successor? on brothers? But will France which has consented to be governed by Joseph or Lucien? Shall I nominate you consul, Cambceres? You? Dare you undertake such a task? And then the will of Louis XIV was not respected; it is likely that mine would be? A dead man, let him be who he will, is nobody." In opposition to all urgency, he ordered the second question to be erased, and the first only to be submitted to the people. It is impossible to divine the motive which influenced Napoleon in the most unexpected decision. Some have supposed that even then he had in view the Empire and the hereditary monarchy, and that he wished to leave a chasm in the organization of the government, as a reason for future change. Others have supposed that he dreaded the rivalries which would arise among his brothers and his nephews, from his having his disposal so resplendent a gift as the Empire of France. But the historian treads upon dangerous ground, when he begins to judge of motives. That which Napoleon actually did was moderate and noble in the highest degree. He declined the power of appointing his successor, and submitted his election to the suffrages of the people. A majority of 3,568,885 voted for the Consulate for life, and only eight thousands and a few hundreds, against it. Never before, or since, was an early government established by such unamitity. Never had a monarch a more indisputable title to his throne. Upon this occasion Lafayette added to his vote these or qualifying words: "I can not vote for such a magistracy, until public freed sufficiently guarantied. When that is done, I give my voice to Napoleon Bonaparte." In a private conversation with the First Consul, he added: "A free government, and you at its head-that comprehends all my desires." Napoleon remarked: In theory Lafayette is perhaps right. But what is theory? A mere dream, when applied to the masses of mankind. He think he is still in the United States--as if the French were Americans. He has no conception of what is required for this country."

A day was fixed for a grand diplomatic festival, when Napoleon should receive the congratulations of the constituted authorities, and of the foreign embassadors. The soldiers, in brilliant uniform, formed a double line, from the Tuileries to the Luxembourg. The First Consul was seated in a magnificent chariot, drawn by eight horses. A cortege of gorgeous splendor accompanied him. All Paris thronged the streets through which he passed, and the most enthusiastic applause rent the heavens. To the congratulatory address of the Senate, Napoleon replied: "The life of a citizen belongs to his country. The French nation wishes that mine should be wholly consecrated to France. I obey its will. Through my efforts, by your assistance, citizen-senators, by the aid of the authorities, and by the confidence and support of this mighty people, the liberty, equality and prosperity of France will be rendered secure against the caprices of fate, and the uncertainty of futurity. The most virtuous of nations will be the most happy, as it deserves to be; and its felicity will contribute to the general happiness of all Europe. Proud then of being thus called, by the command of that Power from which every thing emanates, to bring back order, justice, and equality to the earth, when my last hour approaches, I shall yield myself up with resignation, and, without any solicitude respecting the opinions of future generations."

On the following day the new articles, modifying the constitution in accordance with the change in the consulship, were submitted to the Council of State. The First Consul presided, and with his accustomed vigor and perspicuity, explained the reasons of each article, as he recounted them one by one. The articles contained the provision that Napoleon should nominate his successor to the Senate. To this, after a slight resistance, he yielded, The most profound satisfaction now pervaded France. Even Josephine began to be tranquil and happy She imagined that all thoughts of royalty and of hereditary succession had now passed away. She contemplated with no uneasiness the power which Napoleon sympathized cordially with her in her high gratification that Hortense was soon to become a mother. This child was already, in their hearts, the selected heir to the power of Napoleon. On the 15th of August, Paris magnificiently celebrated the anniversary of the birth-day of the First Consul. This was another introduction of monarchical usages. All the high authorities of the Church and the State, and the foreign diplomatic bodies, called upon him with congratulations. At noon, in all the churches of the metropolis, a Te Deun was sung, in gratitude to God for the gift of Napoleon. At night the city blazed with illuminations. The splendors and the etiquette of royalty were now rapidly introduced; and the same fickle populace who had so recently trampled princes and thrones into blood and ruin, were now captivated with re-introduction of these discarded splendors. Napoleon soon established himself in the beautiful chateau of St. Cloud, which he has caused to be repaired with great magnificence. On the Sabbath the First Consul, with Josephine, invariably attended divine service. Their example was soon followed by most of the members of the court, and the nation as a body returned to Christianity, which, even in its most corrupt form, saves humanity from those abysses of degradation into which infidelity plunges it. Immediately after divine service he conversed in the gallery of the chateau with the visitors who were then waiting for him. The brilliance of his intellect, and his high renown, caused him to be approached with emotions of awe. His words were listened to with intensest eagerness. He was the exclusive object of observation and attention. No earthly potentate had ever attained such a degree of homage, pure and sincere, as now circled around the First Consul.

Napoleon was very desirous of having his court a model of decorum and of morals. Lucien owned a beautiful rural mansion near Neuilly. Upon one occasion he invited Napoleon, and all the inmates of Malmaison, to attend some private theatricals at his dwelling. Lucien and Eliza were the performers in a piece called Alzire. The ardor of their declamation, the freedom of their gestures, and above all the indelicacy of the costume which they assumed, displeased Napoleon exceedingly. As soon as the play was over he exclaimed, "It is a scandal. I ought not to suffer such indecencies. I will give Lucien to understand that I will have no more of it." As soon as Lucien entered the saloon, having resumed his usual dress, Napoleon addressed him before the whole company, and requested him in future to desist from all such representations. "What!" said he, "when I am endeavoring to restore purity of manners, my brother and sister must needs exhibit themselves upon a platform, almost in a state of nudity! It is an insult!"

One day at this time Bourrienne, going from Malmaison to Ruel, lost a beautiful watch. He proclaimed his loss by means of the bellman at Ruel. An hour after, as he was sitting down to dinner, a peasant boy brought him the watch, which he had found on the road. Napoleon heard of the occurrence.

Immediately he instituted inquiries respecting the young man and the family. Hearing a good report of them, he gave the three brothers employment, and amply rewarded the honest lad. "Kindness," says Bourrienne, "was a very prominent trait in the character of Napoleon."

If we now take a brief review of what Napoleon had accomplished since his return from Egypt, it must be admitted that the records of the world are to be searched in vain for a similar recital. No mortal man before ever accomplished so much, or accomplished it so well, in so short a time.

Let us for a moment return to his landing at Frejus on the 8th of October, 1799, until he was chosen First Consul for life, in August, 1802, a period of not quite three years. Proceeding to Paris, almost alone, he overthrew the Directory, and seized the supreme power; restored order into the administration of government, established a new and very efficient system for the collection of taxes, raised public credit, and supplied the wants of the suffering army. By great energy and humanity he immediately terminated the horrors of that unnatural war which had for years, been desolating La Vendee. Condescending to the attitude of suppliant, he implored of Europe peace. Europe chose war. By a majestic conception of military combinations, he sent Moreau with a vast army to the Rhime; stimulated Massena to the most desperate strife at Genoa, and then, creating as by magic, an army, from materials which excited but the ridicule of his foes, he climbed, with artillery and horse, and all the munitions of war, the icy pinnacles of the Alps, and fell like an avalanche upon his foes upon the plain of Marengo. With far inferior numbers, he snatched the victory from the victors; and in the exultant hour of the most signal conquest, wrote again from the field of blood imploring peace. His foes, humbled, and at his mercy, gladly availed themselves of his clemency, and promised to treat. Perfidiously, they only sought time to regain their strength. He then sent Moreau to Hohenlinden, and beneath the walls of Vienna extorted peace with continental Europe. England still prosecuted the war. The first Consul, by his genius, won the heart of Paul of Russia, secured the affection of Prussia, Denmark, and Sweden, and formed a league of all Europe against the Mistress of the Seas. While engaged in this work, he paid the creditors of the State, established the Bank of France, overwhelmed the highway robbers with utter destruction, and restored security in all the provinces; cut magnificent communications over the Alps, founded hospitals on their summits, surrounded exposed cities with fortifications, opened canals, constructed bridges, created magnificent roads, and commenced the compilation of that civil code which will remain an ever-during monument of his labors and his genius. In opposition to the remonstrances of his best friends, he re-established Christianity, and with it proclaimed perfect liberty of conscience. Public works were every where established, to encourage industry. Schools and colleges were founded Merit of every kind was stimulated by abundant rewards. Vast improvements were made in Paris, and the streets cleaned and irrigated. In the midst of all these cares, he was defending France against the assaults of the most powerful nation on the globe; and he was preparing, as his last resort, a vast army, to carry the war into the heart of England. Notwithstanding the most atrocious libels with which England was filled against him, his fame shone resplendent through them all, and he was popular with the English people. Many of the most illustrious of the English statesmen advocated his cause. His gigantic adversary, William Pitt. vanquished by the genius of Napoleon, was compelled to retire from the ministry--and the world was at peace.

The difficulties, perplexities, embarrassments which were encountered in those enterprises, were infinite. Says Napoleon, with that magnanimity which history should recognize and applaud, "We are told that all the First Consul has to look to, was to do justice. But to whom was he to do justice? To the proprietors whom the revolution had violently despoiled of their properties, for this only, that they had been faithful to their legitimate sovereign to the principle of honor which they had inherited from their ancestors; or to those new proprietors, who had purchased these domains, adventuring their money on the faith of laws flowing from an illegitimate authority? Was he to do justice to those royalist soldiers, mutilated in the fields of Germany, La Vendee, and Quiberon, arrayed under the white standard of the Bourbons, in the firm belief that they were serving the cause of their king against a usurping tyranny; or to the million of citizens, who, forming around the frontiers a wall of brass, had so often saved their country from the inveterate hostility of its enemies, and had borne to so transcendent a height the glory of the French eagle? Was he to do justice to that clergy, the model and the example of every Christian virtue, stripped of its birthright, the reward of fifteen hundred years of benevolence; or to the recent acquires, who had converted the convents into workshops, the churches into warehouses, and had turned to profane uses all that had been deemed most holy for ages?"

"At this period," says Theirs, "Napoleon appeared so moderate, after having been so victorious, he showed himself so profound a legislator, after having proved himself so great a commander, he evinced so much love for the arts of peace, after having excelled in the arts of war, that well might he excite illusions in France and in the world. Only some few among the parsonages who were admitted to his councils, who were capable of judging futurity by the present, were filled with as much anxiety as admiration, on witnessing the indefatigable activity of his mind and body, and the energy of his will, and the impetuosity of his desires. They trembled even at seeing him do good, in the way he did--so impatient was he to accomplish it quickly, and upon an immense scale. The wise and sagacious Tronchet, who both admired and loved him, and looked upon him as the savior of France, said, nevertheless, one day in a tone of deep feeling to Cambracers, 'This young man begins like Caesar: I fear that he will end like him.'"

The elevation of Napoleon to the supreme power for life was regarded by most of the states of continental Europe with satisfaction, as tending to diminish the dreaded influences of republicanism, and to assimilate France with the surrounding monarchies. Even in England, the prime Minister, Mr. Addington, assured the French embassador of the cordial approbation of the British government of an event, destined to consolidate order and power in France. The King of Prussia, the Emperor Alexander, and the Archduke Charles of Austria, sent him their friendly congratulations. Even Catharine, the haughty Queen of Naples, mother of the Empress of Austria, being then at Vienna, in ardent expression of her gratification to the French embassador said, "General Bonaparte is a great man. He has done me much injury, but that shall not prevent me from acknowledging his genius. By checking disorder in France, he has rendered a service to all of Europe. He has attained the government of his country because he is most worthy of it. I hold him out every day as a pattern to the young princes of the imperial family. I exhort them to study that extraordinary personage, to learn from him how to direct nations, how to make the yoke of authority endurable, by means of genius and glory."

But difficulties were rapidly rising between England and France. The English were much disappointed in not finding that sale of their manufactures which they had anticipated. The cotton and iron manufactures were the richest branches of industry in England. Napoleon, supremely devoted to the development of the manufacturing resources of France, encouraged those manufactures by the almost absolute prohibition of the rival articles. William Pitt and his partisans, still retaining immense influence, regarded with extreme jealousy the rapid strides which Napoleon was making to power, and incessantly declaimed, in the journals, against the ambition of France. Most of the royalist emigrants, who had refused to acknowledge the new government, and were still devoted to the cause of the Bourbons, had taken refuge in London. They had been the allies with England in the long war against France. The English government could not refrain from sympathizing with them in their sufferings. It would have been ungenerous not to have done so. The emigrants were many of them supported by pensions paid them by England. At the same time they were constantly plotting conspiracies against the life of Napoleon, and sending assassins to shoot him. "I will yet teach those Bourbons," that I am not a man to be shot at like a dog." Napoleon complained bitterly that his enemies, then attempting his assassination, were in the pay of the British government. Almost daily the plots of these emigrants were brought to light by the vigilance of the French police.

A Bourbon pamphleteer, named Peltier, circulated widely through England the most atrocious libels against the First Consul, his wife, her children, his brothers and sisters. They were charged with the most low, degrading, and revolting vices. These accusations were circulated widely through England and

America. They produced a profound impression. They were believed. Many were interested in the circulation of these reports, wishing to destroy the popularity of Napoleon, and to prepare the populace of England for the renewal of the war. Napoleon remonstrated against such infamous representations of his character being allowed in England. But he was informed that the British press was free; that there was no resource but to prosecute for libel in the British courts; and that it was the part of true greatness to treat such slanders with contempt. But Napoleon felt that such false charges were exasperating nations, were paving the way to deluge Europe again in war, and that causes tending to such woes were too potent to be despised.

The Algerines were now sweeping with their paretic crafts the Mediterranean, exacting tribute from all Christian powers. A French ship had been wrecked upon the coast, and the crew were made prisoners. Two French vessels and a Neapolitan ship had also been captured and taken to Algiers. The indignation of Napoleon was aroused. He sent an officer to the Dey with a letter, informing him that if the prisoners were not released and the captured vessels instantly restored, and promise given to respect in future the flags of France and Italy, he would send a fleet and an army and overwhelm him with ruin. The Dey had heard of Napoleon's career in Egypt. He was thoroughly frightened, restored the ships and the prisoners, implored clemency, and with barbarian injustice doomed to death those who had captured the ships in obedience to his commands. Their lives were saved only through the intercession of the French minister Napoleon then performed one of the most gracious acts of courtesy toward the Pope. The feeble monarch had no means of protecting his coasts from the pirates who still swarmed in those seas. Napoleon selected two fine brigs in the naval arsenal at Toulon, equipped them with great elegance, armed them most effectively, filled them with naval stores, and conferring upon them the apostolical names of St. Peter and St. Paul, sent them as a present to the Pontiff. With characteristic grandeur of action, he carried his attentions so far as to send a cutter to bring back the crews, that the papal treasury might be exposed to no expense. The venerable Pope, in the exuberance of his gratitude, insisted upon, taking the French seamen to Rome. He treated them with every attention in his power; exhibited to them St. Peter's, and dazzled them with the pomp and splendor of cathedral worship. They returned to France loaded with humble presents, and exceedingly gratified with the kindness with which they had been received.

It was stipulated in the treaty of Amiens, that both England and France should evacuate Egypt, and that England should surrender Malta to its ancient rulers. Malta, impregnable in its fortifications, commanded the Mediterranean, and was the key of Egypt. Napoleon had therefore, while he professed a willingness to relinquish all claim to the island himself, insisted upon it, as an essential point, that England should do the same. The question upon which the treaty hinged, was the surrender of Malta to a neutral power. The treaty was signed. Napoleon promptly and scrupulously fulfilled his agreements. Several embarrassments, for which England was not responsible, delayed for a few months the evacuation of Malta. But now nearly a year had passed since the signing of the treaty. All obstacles were removed from the way of its entire fulfillment, and yet the troops of England remained both in Egypt and in Malta. The question was seriously discussed in Parliament and in the English journals, whether England were bound to fulfill her engagements, since France was growing so alarmingly powerful. Generously and eloquently Fox exclaimed, "I am astonished at all I hear, particularly when I consider who they are that speak such words. Indeed I am more grieved than any of the honorable friends and colleagues of Mr. Pitt, at the growing greatness of France, which is daily extending her power in Europe and in America. That France, now accused of interfering with the concerns of others, we invaded, for the purpose of forcing upon her a government to which she would not submit, and of obliging her to accept the family of the Bourbons, whose yoke she spurned. By one of those sublime movements, which history should recommend to imitation, and preserve in eternal memorial, she repelled her invaders. Though warmly attached to the cause of England, we have felt an involuntary movement of sympathy with that generous outburst of liberty, and we have no desire to conceal it. No doubt France is great, much greater than a good Englishman ought to wish, but that ought not to be a motive for violating solemn treaties. But because France now appears too great to us--greater than we thought her at first--to break a solemn engagement, to retain Malta, for instance, would be an unworthy breach of faith, which would compromise the honor of Britain. I am sure that if there were in Paris an assembly similar to that which is debating here, the British navy and its dominion over the seas would he talked of, in the same terms as we talk in this house of the French armies, and their dominion over the land."

Napoleon sincerely wished for peace. He was constructing vast works to embellish and improve the empire. Thousands of workmen were employed in cutting magnificent roads across the Alps. He was watching with intensest interest the growth of fortifications and the excavation of canals. He was in the possession of absolute power, was surrounded by universal admiration, and, in the enjoyment of profound peace, was congratulating himself upon being the pacificator of Europe. He had disbanded his armies, and was consecrating all the resources of the nation to the stimulation of industry. He therefore left no means of forbearance and conciliation untried to avert the calamities of war. He received Lord Whitworth, the English embassador in Paris, with great distinction. The most delicate attentions were paid to this lady, the Duchess of Dorset. Splendid entertainments were given at the Tuileries and at St. Cloud in their honor. Talleyrand consecrated to them all the resources of his courtly and elegant manners. The two Associate Consuls, Cambaceres and Lebrum, were also unwearied in attentions. Still all these efforts on the part of Napoleon to secure friendly relations with England were unavailing. The British government still, in open violation of the treaty, retained Malta. The honor of France was at stake in enforcing the sacredness of treaties Malta was too important a post to be left in the hands of England. Napoleon at last resolved to have a personal interview himself with Lord Whitworth, and explain to him, with all frankness, his sentiments and his resolves.

It was on the evening of the 18th of February, 1803, that Napoleon received Lord Whitworth in his cabinet in the Tuileries. A large writing-table occupied the middle of the room. Napoleon invited the embassador to take a seat at one end of the table, and seated himself at the other. "I have wished," said he, "to converse with you in person, that I may fully convince you of my real opinions and intentions." Then with that force of language and that perspicuity which no man ever excelled, he recapitulated his transactions with England from the beginning; that he had offered peace immediately upon the accession to the consulship; that peace had been refused; that eagerly he had renewed negotiations as soon as he could with any propriety do so: and that he had made great concessions to secure the peace of Amiens. "But my efforts," said he, "to live on good terms with England, have met with no friendly response. The English newspapers breathe but animosity against me. The journals of the emigrants are allowed a license of abuse which is not justified by the British constitution. Pensions are granted to Georges and his accomplices, who are plotting my assassination. The emigrants, protected in England, are continually making excursions to France to stir up civil war. The Bourbon princes are received with the insignia of the ancient royalty. Agents are sent to Switzerland and Italy to raise up difficulties against France. Every wind which blows from England brings me but hatred and insult. Now we have come to a situation from which we must relieve ourselves. Will you or will you not execute the treaty of Amiens? I have executed it on my part with scrupulous fidelity. That treaty obliged me to evacuate Naples, Tarento, and the Roman States, within three months. In less than two months, all the French troops were out of those countries. Ten months have elapsed since the exchange of the ratifications, and the English troops are still in Malta, and at Alexandria. It is useless to try to deceive us on this point. Will you have peace, or will you have war? If you are for war, only say so; we will wage it unrelentingly. If you wish for peace, you must evacuate Alexandria and Malta. The rock of Malta, on which so many fortifications have been erected, is, in a maritime point of view, an object of great importance infinitely greater, inasmuch as it implicates the honor of France. What would the world say, if we were to allow a solemn treaty, signed with us, to be violated! It would doubt our energy. For my part, my resolution is fixed. I had rather see you in possession of the Heights of Montmartre, than in possession of Malta."

"If you doubt my desire to preserve peace, listen, and judge how far I am sincere. Though yet very young, I have attained a power, a renown to which it would be difficult to add. Do you imagine that I am solicitous to risk this power, this renown, in a desperate struggle? If I have a war with Austria. I shall contrive to find the way to Vienna. If I have a war with you, I will take from you every ally upon the Continent. You will blockade us; but I will blockade you in my turn. You will make the Continent a prison for us; but I will make the seas a prison for you. However, to conclude the war, there must be more direct efficiency. There must be assembled 150,000 men, and an immense flotilla. We must try to cross the Strait, and perhaps I shall bury in the depths of the sea my fortune, my glory, my life. It is an awful temerity, my lord, the invasion of England." Here, to the amazement of Lord Whitworth, Napoleon enumerated frankly and powerfully all the perils of the enterprise: the enormous preparations it would be necessary to make of ships, men, and munitions of war-the difficulty of eluding the English fleet. "The chance that we shall perish," said he, "is vastly greater than the chance that we shall succeed . Yet this temerity, my lord, awful as it is, I am determined to hazard, if you force me to it. I will risk my army and my life. With me that great enterprise will have chances which it can not have with any other. See now if I ought, prosperous, powerful, and peaceful as I now am, to risk power, prosperity, and peace in such an enterprise. Judge, if when I say I am desirous of peace, if I am not sincere. It is better for you; it is better for me to keep within the limits of treaties. You must evacuate Malta. You must not harbor my assassins in England. Let me be abused, if you please, by the English journals, but not by those miserable emigrants, who dishonor the protection you grant them, and whom the Alien Act permits you to expel from the country. Act cordially with me, and I promise you, on my part, an entire cordiality. See what power we should exercise over the world, if we could bring our two nations together. You have a navy, which, with the incessant efforts of ten years, in the employment of all resources, I should not be able to equal. But I have 500,000 men ready to march, under my command, whithersoever I choose to lead them. If you are masters of the seas, I am master of the land. Let us then think of uniting, rather than of going to war, and we shall rule at pleasure the destinies of the world France and England united, can do every thing for the interests of humanity."

England, however, still refused, upon one pretense and another, to yield

Malta; and both parties were growing more and more exasperated, and were gradually preparing for the renewal of hostilities. Napoleon, at times, gave very free utterance to his indignation. "Malta," said he, "gives the dominion of the Mediterranean. Nobody will believe that I consent to surrender the Mediterranean to the English, unless I fear their power. I thus loose the most important sea in the world, and the respect of Europe. I will fight to the last, for the possession of the Mediterranean; and if I once get to Dover, it is all over with those tyrants of the seas. Besides, as we must fight, sooner or later, with a people to whom the greatness of France is intolerable, the sooner the better. I am young. The English are in the wrong; more so than they will ever be again. I had rather settle the matter at once. They shall not have Malta."

Still Napoleon assented to the proposal for negotiating with the English for the cession of some other island in the Mediterranean. "Let them obtain a port to put into," said he. "To that I have no objection. But I am determined that they shall not have two Gibraltars in that sea, one at the entrance, and one in the middle." To this proposition, however, England refused assent.

Napoleon then proposed that the Island of Malta should be placed in the hands of the Emperor of Russia; leaving it with him in trust, till the discussions between France and England were decided. It had so happened that the emperor had just offered his mediation, if that could be available, to prevent a war. This the English government also declined, upon the plea that it did not think that Russia would be willing to accept the office thus imposed upon her. The English embassador now received instructions to demand that France should cede to England, Malta for ten years; and that England, by way of compensation, would recognize the Italian republic. The embassador was ordered to apply for his passports, if these conditions were not accepted within seven days. To this proposition France would not accede. The English minister demanded his passports, and left France. Immediately the English fleet commenced its attack upon French merchant-ships, wherever they could be found. And the world was again deluged in war.

France has recorded her past history and her present condition, in the regal palaces she has reared. Upon these monumental walls are inscribed, in letters more legible than the hieroglyphics of Egypt, and as ineffaceable, the long and dreary story of kingly vice, voluptuousness and pride, and of popular servility and oppression. The unthinking tourist saunters through these magnificent saloons, upon which have been lavished the wealth of princes and the toil of ages, and admires their gorgeous grandeur. In marbled floors and gilded ceilings and damask tapestry, and all the appliances of boundless luxury and opulence, he sees but the triumphs of art, and bewildered by the dazzling spectacle, forgets the burning outrage upon human rights which it proclaims. Half-entranced, he wanders through uncounted acres of groves and lawns, and parterres of flowers, embellished with lakes, fountains, cascades, and the most voluptuous statuary, where kings and queens have reveled, and he reflects not upon the millions who have toiled, from dewy morn till the shades of night, through long and joyless years, eating black bread, clothed in coarse raiment-- the man, the woman, the ox, companions in toil, companions in thought--to minister to this indulgence. But the palaces of France proclaim, in trumpet tones, the shame of France. They say to her kings. Behold the undeniable monuments of your pride, your insatiate extortion, your measureless extravagance and luxury. They say to the people, Behold the proofs of the outrages which your fathers, for countless ages, have endured. They lived in mud hovels that their licentious kings might riot haughtily in the apartments, canopied with gold, of Versailles, the Tuileries, and St. Cloud--the Palaces of France. The mind of the political economist lingers painfully upon them. They are gorgeous as specimens of art. They are sacred as memorials of the past. Vandalism alone would raze them to their foundations. Still, the judgment says, It would be better for the political regeneration of France, if, like the Bastile, their very foundations were plowed up, and sown with salt. For they are a perpetual provocative to every thinking man. They excite unceasingly democratic rage against aristocratic arrogance. Thousands of noble women, as they traverse those gorgeous halls, feel those fires of indignation glowing in their souls, which glowed in the bosom of Madame Roland. Thousands of young men, with compressed lip and moistened eye, lean against those marble pillars, lost in thought, and almost excuse even the demoniac and blood-thirsty mercilessness of Danton, Marat, and Robespierre. These palaces are a perpetual stimulus and provocative to governmental aggression. There they stand, in all their gorgeousness, empty, swept, and garnished. They are resplendently beautiful. They are supplied with every convenience, every luxury. King and Emperor dwelt there. Why should not the President ? Hence the palace becomes the home of the Republican President. The expenses of the palace, the retinue of the palace, the court etiquette of the palace become the requisitions of good taste. In America, the head of the government, in his convenient and appropriate mansion, receives a salary of twenty-five thousand dollars a year. In France, the President of the Republic receives four hundred thousand dollars a year, and yet, even with that vast sum, can not keep up an establishment at all in accordance with the dwellings of grandeur which invite his occupancy, and which unceasingly and irresistibly stimulate to regal pomp and to regal extravagance. The palaces of France have a vast influence upon the present politics of France. There is an unceasing conflict between those marble walls of monarchical splendor, and the principles of republican simplicity. This contest will not soon terminate, and its result no one can foresee. Never have I felt my indignation more thoroughly aroused than when wandering hour after hour through the voluptuous sumptuousness of Versailles. The triumphs of taste and art are admirable, beyond the power of the pen to describe. But the moral of exeerable oppression is deeply inscribed upon all. In a brief description of the Palaces of France. I shall present them in the order in which I chanced to visit them.

1. Palais des Thermes .--In long-gone centuries, which have faded away into oblivion, a wandering tribe of barbarians alighted from their canoes, upon a small island in the Seine, and there reared their huts. They were called the Parisii. The slow lapse of centuries rolled over them, and there were wars and woes, bridals and burials, and still they increased in numbers and in strength, and fortified their little isle against the invasions of their enemies; for man, whether civilized or savage, has ever been the most ferocious wild beast man has had to encounter. But soon the tramp of the Roman legions was heard upon the banks of the Seine, and all Gaul with its sixty tribes, came under the power of the Caesars. Extensive marshes and gloomy forests surrounded the barbarian village; but, gradually, Roman laws and institutions were introduced;

and Roman energy changed the aspect of the country. Immediately the proud conquerors commenced rearing a palace for the provincial governor. The Palace of Warm Baths rose, with its massive walls and in imposing grandeur. Roman spears drove the people to the work; and Roman ingenuity knew well how to extort from the populace the revenue which was required. Large remains of that palace continue to the present day. It is the most interesting memorial of the past which can now be found in France. The magnificence of its proportions still strike the beholder with awe. "Behold," says a writer, who trod its marble floors nearly a thousand years ago: "Behold the Palace of the Kings, whose turrets pierce the skies, and whose foundations penetrate even to the empire of the dead." Julius Caesar gazed proudly upon those turrets; and here the shouts of Roman legions, fifteen hundred years ago proclaimed Julian emperor; and Roman maidens, with throbbing hearts, trod these floors in the mazy dance. No one can enter the grand hall of the haths, without being deeply impressed with the majestic aspect of the edifice, and with the grandeur of its gigantic proportions. The decay of nearly two thousand years has left its venerable impress upon those walls. Here Roman generals proudly strode, encased in brass and steel, and the clatter of their arms resounded through these arches. In these mouldering, crumbling tubs of stone, they laved their sinewy limbs. But where are those fierce warriors now? In what employments have their turbulent spirits been engaged, while generation after generation has passed on earth, in the enactment of the comedies and the tragedies of life? Did their rough tutelage in the camp, and their proud hearing in the court, prepare them for the love, the kindness, the gentleness, the devotion of Heaven? In fields of outrage, clamor, and blood, madly rushing to the assault, shouting in frenzy, dealing, with iron hand, every where around, destruction and death, did they acquire a taste for the "green pastures and the still waters?" Alas! for the mystery of our being! They are gone, and gone forever! Their name has perished--their language is forgotten.

"The storm which wrecks the wintry sky. No more disturbs their deep repose, Than summer evening's gentlest sign, Which shuts the rose."

Upon a part of the rums of this old palace of Caesars, there has been reared by more modern ancients , still another palace, where mirth and revelry have resounded, where pride has elevated her haughty head, and vanity displayed her costly robes--but over all those scenes of splendor, death has rolled its oblivious waves. About four hundred years ago, upon a portion of the crumbling walls of this old Roman mansion, the Palace of Cluny was reared. For three centuries, this palace was one of the abodes of the kings of France. The tide of regal life ebbed and flowed through those saloons, and along those corridors. There is the chamber where Mary of England, sister of Henry VIII., and widow of Louis XII., passed the weary years of her widowhood. It is still called the chamber of the "white queen," from the custom of the queens of France to wear white mourning. Three hundred years ago, these Gothic turrets, and gorgeously ornamented lucarne windows, gleamed with illuminations, as the young King of Scotland, James V., led Madeleine, the blooming daughter of Francis I., to the bridal altar. Here the haughty family of the Guises ostentatiously displayed their regal retinue--vying with the Kings of France in splendor, and outvying them in power. These two palaces, now blended by the nuptails of decay into one, are converted into a museum of antiquities--silent despositories of memorials of the dead. Sadly one loiters through their deserted halls. They present one of the most interesting sights of Paris. In the reflective mind they awaken emotions which the pen can not describe.

2. The Lourre .--When Paris consisted only of the little island in the Seine, and kings and feudal lords, with wine and wassail were reveling in the saloons of China, a hunting-seat was reared in the the dense forest which spread itself along the banks of the river. As the city extended, and the forest disappeared, the hunting-seat was enlarged, strengthened, and became a fortress and a state-prison Thus it continued for three hundred years. In its gloomy dungeons prisoners of state, and the victims of crime, groaned and died; and countless tragedies of despotic power there transpired, which the Day of Judgment alone can reveal. Three hundred years ago, Francis I, tore down the dilapidated walls of this old castle, and commerces the magnificent Palace of the Louver upon their foundations. But its construction has required candle, while Gilpin, who was taller and stronger than either of the other boys, bored the hole in the door, in the place which Rodolphus indicated. When the hole was bored, the boys

inserted an iron rod into it. and running this rod under the hasp, they pried the hasp up and unfastened the door. They opened the door, and then, to their great joy, found themselves all safe in the office.

They put the dark lantern down upon the table, and covered it with its screen, and then listened, perfectly whist, a minute or two, to be sure that nobody was coming.

"You go and watch at the shed-door," said Gilpin to Rodolphus, "while we open the desk."

So Rodolphus went to the shed-door. He peeped out, and looked up and down the village-street, but all was still.

Presently he heard a sort of splitting sound within the office, which he knew was made by the forcing open of the lid of the desk. Very soon afterward the boys came out, in a hurried manner--Griff had the lantern and Gilpin the box.

"Have you got it!" said Rodolphus.

"Yes," said Griff.

"Let's see," said Rodolphus.

Griff held out the box to Rodolphus. It was very heavy and they could hear the sound of the money within. All three of the boys seemed almost wild with trepidation and excitement. Griff however immediately began to hurry them away, pulling the box from them and saying, "Come, come, boys, we must not stay fooling here."

"Wait a minute till I hide the tools again!" said Rodolphus, "and then we'll run."

Rodolphus hid the tools behind the wood-pile, in the shed, where they had been before, and then the boys sallied forth into the street. They crept along stealthily in the shadows of the houses and the most dark and obscure places, until they came to the tavern, where they were to turn down the lane to the corn-barn. As soon as they got safely to this lane, they felt relieved, and they walked on in a more unconcerned manner; and when at length they got fairly in under the corn-barn they felt perfectly secure.

"There," said Griff, "was not that well done!"

"Yes," said Rodolphus, "and now all that we have got to do is to get the box open."

"We can break it open with stones," said Griff.

"No," said Gilpin, "that will make too much noise. We will bury it under this straw for a few days, and open it somehow or other by-and-by, when they have given up looking for the box. You can get the real key of it for us, Rodolphus, can't you!"

"How can I get it?" asked Rodolphus.

"Oh, you can contrive some way to get it from old Kerber, I've no doubt. At any rate the best thing is to bury it now.'

To this plan the boys all agreed. They pulled away the straw, which was spread under the corn-barn, and dug a hole in the ground beneath, working partly with sticks and partly with their fingers. When they had got the hole deep enough, they put the box in and covered it up. Then they covered it up. Then they spread the straw over the place as before.

During all this time the lantern had been standing upon a box pretty near by, having been put there by the boys, in order that the light might shine down upon the place where they had been digging. As soon as their work was done, the boys went softly outside to see if the way was clear for them to go home, leaving the lantern on the box; and while they were standing at the corner of the barn outside, looking up the lane, and whispering together, they saw suddenly a light beginning to gleam up from within. They ran in and found that the lantern had fallen down, and that the straw was all in a blaze. They immediately began to tread upon the fire and try to put it out, but the instant that they did so they were all thunderstruck by the appearance of a fourth person, who came rushing in among them from the outside. They all screamed out with terror and ran. Rodolphus separated from the rest and crouched down a moment behind the stone wall, but immediately afterward, feeling that there would be no safety for him here, he set off again and ran across some back fields and gardens, in the direction toward Mr. Kerber's. He looked back occasionally and found that the light was rapidly increasing. Presently he began to hear cries of fire. He ran on till he reached the house; he scrambled over the fences into the back yard, climbed up upon a shed, crept along under the chimneys to the window of his room, got in as fast as he could, undressed himself and went to bed, and had just drawn the clothes up over him, when he heard a loud knocking at the door, and Mrs. Kerber's voice outside, calling out to him, that there was a cry of fire in the village, and that he must get up quick as possible and help put it out.

The Expedition to Egypt was one of the most magnificent enterprises which human ambition ever conceived. The Return to France combines still more, if possible, of the elements of the moral sublime. But for the disastrous destruction of the French fleet the plans of Napoleon, in reference to the East, would probably have been triumphantly successful. At least it can not be doubted that a vast change would have been effected throughout the Eastern world. Those plans were now hopeless. The army was isolated, and cut off from all reinforcements and all supplies. the best thing which Napoleon could do for his troops in Egypt was to return to France, and exert his personal influence in sending them succor. His return involved the continuance of the most honorable devotion to those soldiers whom he necessarily left behind him. The secrecy of his departure was essential to its success. Had the bold attempt been suspected, it would certainly have been frustrated by the increased vigilance of the English cruisers. The intrepidity of the enterprise must elicit universal admiration.

Contemplate, for a moment, the moral aspects of this undertaking. A nation of thirty millions of people, had been for ten years agitated by the most terrible convulsions. There is no atrocity, which the tongue can name, which had not desolated the doomed land. Every passion which can degrade the heart of fallen man, had swept with simoom blast over the cities and the villages of France. Conflagrations had laid the palaces of the wealthy in ruins, and the green lawns where their children had played, had been crimsoned with the blood of fathers and sons, mothers and daughters. A gigantic system of robbery had seized upon houses and lands and every species of property and had turned thousands of the opulent out into destitution, beggary, and death. Pollution had been legalized by the voice of God-defying lust, and France, la belle France , had been converted into a disgusting warehouse of infamy. Law, with suicidal hand, had destroyed itself, and the decisions of the legislature swayed to and fro, in accordance with the hideous clamors of the mob. The guillotine, with gutters ever clotted with human gore, was the only argument which anarchy condescended to use. Effectually it silenced every remonstrating tongue. Constitution after constitution had risen, like mushrooms, in a night, and like mushrooms had perished in a day. Civil war was raging with bloodhound fury in France, Monarchists and Jacobins grappling each other infuriate with despair. The allied kings of Europe, who by their alliance had fanned these flames of rage and ruin, were gazing with terror upon the portentous prodigy, and were surrounding France with their navies and their armies.

The people had been enslaved for centuries by the king and the nobles. Their oppression had been execrable, and it had become absolutely unendurable. "We, the millions," they exclaimed in their rage, "will no longer minister to your voluptuousness, and pride, and lust." "You shall, you insolent dogs," exclaimed king and nobles, "we heed not your barking." "You shall," reiterated the Pope, in the portentous thunderings of the Vatican. "You shall," came echoed back from the palaces of Vienna, from the dome of the Kremlin, from the seraglio of the Turk, and, in tones deeper, stronger, more resolute, from constitutional, liberty-loving, happy England. Then was France a volcano, and its lava-streams deluged Europe. The people were desperate. In the blind fury of their frenzied self-defense they lost all consideration. The castles of the nobles were but the monuments of past taxation and servitude. With yells of hatred the infuriated populace razed them to the ground. The palaces of the kings, where, for uncounted centuries, dissolute monarchs had reveled in enervating and heaven-forbidden pleasures, were but national badges of the bondage of the people. The indignant throng swept through them, like a Mississippi inundation, leaving upon marble floors, and cartooned walls and ceilings, the impress of their rage. At one bound France had passed from despotism to anarchy. The kingly tyrant, with golden crown and iron sceptre, surrounded by wealthy nobles and dissolute beauties, had disappeared, and a many-headed monster, rapacious and blood-thirsty, vulgar and revolting, had emerged from mines and workshops and the cellars of vice and penury, like one of the spectres of fairy tales to fill his place. France had passed from Monarchy, not to healthy Republicanism, but to Jacobinism, to the reign of the mob. Napoleon utterly abhorred the tyranny of the king. He also utterly abhorred the despotism of vulgar, violent, sanguinary Jacobin misrule. The latter he regarded with even far deeper repugnance than the former. "I frankly confess," said Napoleon, again and again, "that if I must choose between Bourbon oppression, and mob violence, I infinitely prefer the former.

Such had been the state of France, essentially, for nearly ten years. The great mass of the people were exhausted with suffering, and longed for repose. The land was filled with plots and counterplots. But there was no one man of sufficient prominence to carry with him the nation. The government was despised and disregarded. France was in a state of chaotic ruin. Many voices here and there, began to inquire "Where is Bonaparte, the conqueror of Italy, the conqueror of Egypt? He alone can save us." His world-wide renown turned the eyes of the nation to him as their only hope.

Under these circumstances Napoleon, then a young man but twenty-nine years of age, and who, but three years before, had been unknown to fame or to fortune, resolved to return to France, to overthrow the miserable government, by which the country was disgraced, to subdue anarchy at home and aggression from abroad, and to rescue thirty millions of people from ruin. The enterprise was undeniably magnificent in its grandeur and noble in its object. He had two foes to encounter, each formidable, the royalists of combined Europe and the mob of Paris. The quiet and undoubting self-confidence with which he entered upon this enterprise, is one of the most remarkable events in the whole of his extraordinay career. He took with him no armies to hew down opposition. He engaged in no deep-laid and wide-spread conspiracy. Relying upon the energies of his own mind, and upon the sympathies of the great mass of the people, he went alone, with but one or two companions, to whom he revealed not his thoughts, to gather into his hands the scattered reins of power. Never did he encounter more fearful peril. The cruisers of England, Russia, Turkey, of allied Europe in arms against France, thronged the Mediterranean. How could he hope to escape them? The guillotine was red with blood. Every one who had dared to oppose the mob had perished upon it. How could Napoleon venture, single-handed, to beard this terrible lion in his den?

It was ten o'clock at night, the 22d of August, 1799, when Napoleon ascended the sides of the frigate Muiron, to France. A few of his faithful Guards, and eight companions, either officers in the army or members of the scientific corps, accompanied him. There were five hundred soldiers on board the ships. The stars shone brightly in the Syrian sky, and under their soft light the blue waves of the Mediterranean lay spread out most peacefully before them. The frigates unfurled their sails. Napoleon, silent and lost in thought, for a long time walked the quarter deck of the ship, gazing upon the low outline of Egypt as, in the dim starlight, it faded away. His companions were intoxicated with delight, in view of again returning to France. Napoleon was neither elated nor depressed. Serene and silent he communed with himself, and whenever we can catch a glimpse of those secret communings we find them always bearing the impress of grandeur. Though Napoleon was in the habit of visiting the soldiers at their camp fires, of sitting down and conversing with them with the greatest freedom and familiarity, the majesty of his character overawed his officers, and adoration and reserve blended with their love. Though there was no haughtiness in his demeanor, he habitually dwelt in a region of elevation above them all. Their talk was of cards, of wine, of pretty women. Napoleon's thoughts were of empire, of renown, of moulding the destinies of nations. They regarded him not as a companion, but as a master, whose wishes they loved to anticipate; for he would surely guide them to wealth, and fame, and fortune. He contemplated them, not as equals and confiding friends, but as efficient and valuable instruments for the accomplishment of his purposes. Murat was to Napoleon a body of ten thousand horsemen, ever ready for a resistless charge. Lannes was a phalanx of infantry, bristling with bayonets, which neither artillery nor cavalry could batter down or break. Augereau was an armed column of invincible troops, black, dense, massy, impetuous, resistless, moving with gigantic tread wherever the finger of the conqueror pointed. These were but the members of Napoleon's body, the limbs obedient to the mighty soul which swayed them. They were not the companions of his thoughts, they were only the servants of his will. The number to be found with whom the soul of Napoleon could dwell in sympathetic friendship was few-- very few.

Napoleon had formed a very low estimate of human nature, and consequently made great allowance for the infirmities incident to humanity. Bourrienne reports him as saying, "Friendship is but a name. I love no one; no, not even my brothers. Joseph perhaps a little. And if I do love him, it is from habit, and because he is my elder. Duroc! Ah, yes! I love him too. But why? His character please me. He is cold, reserved, and resolute, and I really believe that he never shed a tear. As to myself, I know well that I have not one true friend. As long as I continue what I am, I may have as many pretended friends as I please. We must leave sensibility to the women. It is their business. Men should have nothing to do with war or government. I am not amiable. No; I am not amiable. I never have been. But I am just."

In another mood of mind, more tender, more subdued, he remarked, at St. Helena, in reply to Las Casas, who with great severity was condemning those who abandoned Napoleon in his hour of adversity: "You are not acquainted with men. They are difficult to comprehend if one wishes to be strictly just. Can they understand or explain even their own characters? Almost all those who abandoned me would had I continued to be prosperous, never perhaps have dreamed of their own defection. There are vices and virtues which depend upon circumstances. Our last trials were beyond all human strength! Besides I was forsaken rather than betrayed; there was more weakness than of perfidy around me. It was the denial of St. Peter . Tears and penitence are probably at hand. And where will you find in the page of history any one possessing a greater number of friends and partisans? Who was ever more popular and more beloved? Who was ever more ardently and deeply regretted? Here from this very rock on viewing the present disorders in France who would not be tempted to say that I still reign there? No; human nature might have appeared in a more odious light."

Las Casas, who shared with Napoleon his weary years of imprisonment at St. Helena says of him: "He views the complicated circumstances of his from so high a point that individuals escape his notice. He never evinces the least symptom of virulence toward those of whom it might be supposed he has the greatest reason to complain. His strongest mark of reprobation, and I have had frequent occasions to notice it, is to preserve silence with respect to them whenever they are mentioned in his presence. But how often has he been heard to restrain the violent and less reserved expressions of those about him?"

"And here I must observe," say Las Casas, "that since I have become acquainted with the Emperor's character, I have never known him to evince, for a single moment, the least feeling of anger or animosity against those who had most deeply injured him. He speaks of them coolly and without resentment, attributing their conduct in some measure to the place, and throwing the rest to the account of human weakness."

Marmont, who surrendered Paris to the allies was severely condemned by Las Casas. Napoleon replied: "Vanity was his ruin. Posterity will justly cast a shade upon his character, yet his heart will be more valued than the memory of his career." "Your attachment for Berthier," said Las Casas, "surprised us. He was full of pretensions and pride." "Berthier was not with out talent." Napoleon replied, "and I am far from wishing to disavow his merit, or my partiality; but he was so undecided!" He was very harsh and overbearing." Las Casas rejoined. "And what, my dear Las Casas," Napoleon replied, "is more overbearing than weakness which feels itself protected by strength! Look at women for example." This Berthier had with the utmost meanness, abandoned his benefactor, and took his place in front of the carriage of Louis XVIII. as he rode triumphantly into Paris. "The only revenge I wish on this poor Berthier," said Napoleon at the time, "would be to see him in his costume of captain of the body-guard of Louis."

Says Bourrienne, Napoleon's rejected secretary, "The character of Napoleon was not a cruel one. He was neither rancorous nor vindictive. None but those who are blinded by fury, could have given him the name of Nero or Caligula. I think that I have stated his real fault with sufficient sincerity to be believed upon my word. I can assert that Bonaparte, apart from politics, was feeling kind, and accessible to pity. He was very fond of children, and a bad man has seldom that disposition. In the habits of private life he had and the expression is not too strong, much benevolence and great indulgence for human weakness. A contrary opinion is too firmly fixed in some minds for me to hope to remove it. I shall, I fear, have opposers; but I address myself to those who are in search of truth. I lived in the most unreserved confidence with Napoleon until the age of thirty-four years, and I advance nothing lightly." This is the admission of one who had been ejected from office by Napoleon, and who become a courtier of the reinstated Bourbons. It is a candid admission of an enemy.

The ships weighed anchor in the darkness of the night, hoping before the day should dawn to escape the English cruisers which were hovering about Alexandria. Unfortunately, at midnight, the wind died away, and it became almost perfectly calm. Fearful of being captured, some were anxious to seek again the shore. "Be quiet," said Napoleon, "we shall pass in safety."

Admiral Gantheaume wished to take the shortest route to France. Napoleon, however, directed the admiral to sail along as near as possible the coast of Africa, and to continue that unfrequented route, till the ships should pass the Island of Sardinia. "In the mean while," said he, "should an English fleet present itself, we will run ashore upon the sands, and march, with the handful of brave men and the few pieces of artillery we have with us, to Oran or Tunis, and there find means to re-embark." Thus Napoleon, is this hazardous enterprise braved every peril. The most imminent and the most to be dreaded of all was captivity in an English prison. For twenty days the wind was so invariable adverse, that the ships did not advance three hundred miles. Many were so discouraged and so apprehensive of capture that it was even proposed to return to Alexandria. Napoleon was much in the habit of peaceful submission to that which he could not remedy. During all these trying weeks he appeared perfectly serene and contented. To the murmuring of his companions he replied, "We shall arrive in France in safety. I am determined to proceed at all hazards. Fortune will not abandon us." "People frequently speak," says Bourrienne, who accompanied Napoleon upon this voyage, "of the good fortune which attaches to an individual, and even attends him this sort of predestination, yet, when I call to mind the numerous dangers which Bonaparte escaped in so many enterprises, the hazards he encountered, the chances he ran, I can conceive that others may have this faith. But having for a length of time studied the 'man of destiny', I have remarked that what was called his fortune was, in reality, his genius; that his success was the consequence of his admirable foresight--of his calculations, rapid as lightning, and of the conviction that boldness is often the truest wisdom. If, for example, during our voyage from Egypt to France, he had not imperiously insisted upon pursuing a course different from that usually taken, and which usual course was recommended by the admiral, would he have escaped the perils which beset his path! Probably not. And was all this the effect of chance. .... Certainly not."

During these days of suspense Napoleon, apparently as serene in spirit as the calm which often silvered the unrippled surface of the sea held all the energies of his mind in perfect control. A choice library he invariably took with him wherever he went. He devoted the hours to writing study, finding recreation in solving the most difficult problems in geometry, and in investigating chemistry and other scientific subjects of practical utility. He devoted much time to conversation with the distinguished scholars whom he had selected to accompany him. His whole soul seemed engrossed in the pursuit of literary and scientific attainments. He also carefully, and with most intense interest, studied the Bible and Koran, scrutinizing, with the eye of a philosopher, the antagonistic system of the Christian and the Moslem. The limity of the Scriptures charmed him. He read again and again, with deep admiration, Christ's sermon upon the mount and called his companions form their card-tables, to read it to them, that they might also appreciate its moral beauty and its eloquence. "You will ere long, become devout yourself," said one of his infidel companions. "I wish I might become so," Napoleon replied. "What a solace Christianity must be to one who has an undoubting conviction of its truth." But practical Christianity he had only seen in the mummeries of the papal church. Remembering the fasts, the vigils, the penances, the cloisters, the scourgings of a corrupt Christianity, and contrasting them with the voluptuous paradise and the sensual houries which inflamed the eager vision of the Moslem, he once exclaimed in phrase characteristic of his genius, "The religion of Jesus is a threat, that of Mohammed." The religion of Jesus is not a threat. Though the wrath of God shall fall upon the children of disobedience, our Saviour invites us, in gentle accents, to the green pastures and the still waters of the Heavenly Canaan; to cities resplendent with pearls and gold; to mansions of which God is the architect; to the songs of seraphim, and the flight of cherubim, exploring on tireless pinion the wonders of infinity; to peace of conscience and rapture dwelling in pure heart and to blest companionship loving and beloved; to majesty of person and loftiness of intellect; to appear as children and as nobles in the audience-chamber of God; to an immorality of bliss. No! the religion of Jesus is not a threat, though it has too often been thus represented by its mistaken or designing advocates.

One evening a group of officers were conversing together, upon the quarter deck, respecting the existence of God. Many of them believed not in his being. It was a calm, cloudless, brilliant night. The heavens, the work of God's fingers, canopied them gloriously. The moon and the stars, which God had ordained beamed down upon them with serene lustre. As they were flippantly giving utterance to the arguments of atheism. Napoleon paced to and fro upon the deck, taking no part in the conversation, and apparently absorbed in his own thoughts. Suddenly he stopped before them and said, in those tones of dignity which ever overawed, "Gentlemen, your arguments are very fine. But who made all those worlds, beaming so gloriously above us? Can you tell me that?" No one answered. Napoleon resumed his silent walk, and the officers selected another topic for conversation.

 In these intense studies Napoleon first began to appreciate the beauty and the sublimity of Christianity. Previously to this, his own strong sense had taught him the principles of a noble toleration; and Jew, Christian, and Moslem stood equally regarded before him. Now he began to apprehend the surpassing excellence of Christianity. And though the cares of the busiest life through which a mortal has ever passed soon engrossed his energies, this appreciation and admiration of the gospel of Christ, visibly increased with each succeeding year. He unflinchingly braved the scoffs of infidel Europe, in re-establishing the Christian religion in paganized France. He periled his popularity with the army, and disregarded the opposition of his most influential friends, from his deep conviction of the importance of religion to the welfare of the state. With the inimitable force of his own glowing eloquence, he said to Montholon, at St. Helena, "I know men, and I tell you that Jesus Christ is not a man! The religion of Christ is a mystery, which subsists by its own force, and proceeds from a mind which is not a human mind. We find in it a marked individuality which originated a train of words and maxims unknown before. Jesus borrowed nothing from our knowledge. He exhibited himself the perfect example of his precepts. Jesus is not a philosopher: for his proofs are his miracles, and from the first his disciples adored him. In fact, learning and philosophy are of no use for salvation; and Jesus came into the world to reveal the mysteries of heaven and the laws of the spirit. Alexander, Caesar, Charlemagne, and myself have founded empires. But upon what did we rest the creations of our genius? upon force . Jesus Christ alone founded his empire upon love. And at this moment millions of men would die for him. I die before my time, and my body will be given back to earth, to become food for worms. Such is the fate of him who has been called the great Napoleon. What an abyss between my deep misery and the eternal kingdom of Christ, which is proclaimed, loved, and adored, and which is extending over the whole earth!

Call you this dying? Is it not living rather? The death of Christ is the death of a God!"

At the time of the invasion of Egypt, Napoleon regarded all forms of religion with equal respect. And though he considered Christianity superior, in intellectuality and refinement, to all other modes of worship, he did not consider any religion as of divine origin. At one time, speaking of the course which he pursued in Egypt, he said, "Such was the disposition of the army, that in order to induce them to listen to the bare mention of religion, I was obliged to speak very lightly on the subject; to place Jews beside Christians, and rabbis beside bishops. But after all it would not have been so very extraordinary had circumstances induced me to embrace Islamism. But I must have had good reasons for my conversion. I must have been secure of advancing at least as far as the Euphrates. Change of religion for private interest is inexcusable. But it may be pardoned in consideration of immense political results. Henry IV. said, Paris is well worth a mass . Will it then be said that the dominion of the East, and perhaps the subjugation of all Asia, were not worth a turban and a pair of trousers ? And in truth the whole matter was reduced to this. The sheiks had studied how to render it easy to us. They had smoothed down the great obstacles, allowed us the use of wine, and dispensed with all corporeal formalities. We should have lost only our small-clothes and hats."

Of the infidel Rousseau, Napoleon ever spoke in terms of severe reprobation. "He was a bad man, a very bad man," said he, "he caused the revolution." "I was not aware," another replied, "that you considered the French Revolution such an unmixed evil." "Ah," Napoleon rejoined, "you wish to say that without the revolution you would not have had me. Nevertheless, without the revolution France would have been more happy." When invited to visit the hermitage of Rousseau, to see his cap, table, great chair, &c., he exclaimed, "Bah! I have no taste for such fooleries. Show them to my brother Louis. He is worthy of them."

Probably the following remarks of Napoleon, made at St. Helena, will give a very correct idea of his prevailing feeling upon the subject of religion. "The sentiment of religion is so consolatory, that it must be considered a gift from Heaven. What a resource would it not be for us here, to possess it. What rewards have I not a right to expect, who have run a career so extraordinary, so tempestuous, as mine has been, without committing a single crime. And yet how many might I not have been guilty of? I can appear before the tribunal of God, I can await his judgment, without fear. He will not find my conscience stained with the thoughts of murder and poisonings; with the infliction of violent and premeditated deaths, events so common in the history of those whose lives resemble mine. I have wished only for the power, the greatness, the glory of France. All my faculties, all my efforts, all my movements, were directed to the attainment of that object. These can not be crimes. To me they appeared acts of virtue. What then would be my happiness, if the bright prospect of futurity presented itself to crown the last moments of my existence."

After a moment's pause, in which he seemed lost in thought, he resumed: "But, how is it possible that conviction can find its way to our hearts, when we hear the absurd language, and witness the iniquitous conduct of the greater part of those whose business it is to preach to us. I am surrounded by priests, who repeat incessantly that their reign is not of this world; and yet they lay their hands upon every thing which they can get. The Pope is the head of that religion which is from Heaven. What did the present chief pontiff, who is undoubtedly a good and a holy man, not offer, to be allowed to return to Rome. The surrender of the government of the church, of the institution of bishops was not too much for him to give, to become once more a secular prince.

"Nevertheless," he continued, after another thoughtful pause, "it can not be doubted that, as emperor, the species of incredulity which I felt was beneficial to the nations I had to govern. How could I have favored equally sects so opposed to one another, if I had joined any one of them? How could I have preserved the independence of my thoughts and of my actions under the control of a confessor, who would have governed me under the dread of hell!" Napoleon closed this conversation, by ordering the New Testament to be brought. Commencing at the beginning, he read aloud as far as the conclusion of our Savior's address to his disciples upon the mountain. He expressed himself struck with the highest admiration, in contemplating its purity, its sublimity, and the beautiful perfection of its moral code.

For forty days the ships were driven about by contrary winds, and on the 1st of October they made the island of Corsica, and took refuge in the harbor of Ajaccio. The tidings that Napoleon had landed in his native town swept over the island like a gale, and the whole population crowded to the port to catch a sight of their illustrious countryman. "It seemed," said Napoleon, "that half of the inhabitants had discovered traces of kindred." But a few years had elapsed since the dwelling of Madame Letitia was pillaged by the mob, and the whole Bonaparte family, in penury and friendlessness, were hunted from their home, effecting their escape in an open boat by night. Now, the name of Bonaparte filled the island with acclamations. But Napoleon was alike indifferent to such unjust censure, and to such unthinking applause. As the curse did not depress, neither did the hosanna elate.

After the delay of a few days in obtaining supplies, the ships again weighed anchor, on the 7th of October, and continued their perilous voyage. The evening of the next day, as the sun was going down in unusual splendor, there appeared in the west, painted in strong relief against his golden rays, an English squadron. The admiral, who saw from the enemy's signals that he was observed, urged an immediate return to Corsica. Napoleon, convinced that capture would be the result of such a manoeuvre, exclaimed, "To do so would be to take the road to England.

I am seeking that to France. Spread all sail. Let every one be at his post. Steer to the northwest. Onward." The night was dark, the wind fair. Rapidly the ships were approaching the coast of France, through the midst of the hostile squadron, and exposed to the most imminent danger of capture. Escape seemed impossible. It was a night of fearful apprehension and terror to all on board, excepting Napoleon. He determined, in case of extremity, to throw himself into a boat, and trust for safety to darkness and the oars. With the most perfect self-possession and composure of spirits, he ordered the long-boat to be prepared, selected those whom he desired to accompany him, and carefully collected such papers as he was anxious to preserve. Not an eye was closed during the night. It was indeed a fearful question to be decided. Are these weary wanderers, in a few hours, to be in the embrace of their wives and their children, or will the next moment show them the black hull of an English man-of war, emerging from the gloom, to consign them to lingering years of captivity in an English prison? In this terrible hour no one could perceive that the composure of Napoleon was in the slightest degree ruffled. The first drawn of the morning revealed to their straining vision the hills of France stretching along but a few leagues before them, and far away, in the northeast, the hostile squadron, disappearing beneath the horizon of the sea. The French had escaped. The wildest bursts of joy rose from the ships. But Napoleon gazed calmly upon his beloved France, with pale cheek and marble brow, too proud to manifest emotion. At eight o'clock in the morning the four vessels dropped anchor in the little harbor of Frejus. It was the morning of the 8th of October. Thus for fifty days Napoleon had been tossed upon the waves of the Mediterranean, surrounded by the hostile flects of England, Russia, and Turkey, and yet had eluded their vigilance.

This wonderful passage of Napoleon, gave rise to many caricatures, both in England and France. One of these caricatures, which was conspicuous in the London shop windows, possessed so much point and historic truth, that Napoleon is said to have laughed most heartily on seeing it. Lord Nelson, as is well known, with all his heroism, was not exempt from the frailties of humanity. The British admiral was represented as guarding Napoleon. Lady Hamilton makes her appearance, and his lordship becomes so engrossed in caressing the fair enchantress, that Napoleon escapes between his legs. This was hardly a caricature. It was almost historic verity. While Napoleon was struggling against adverse storms off the coast of Africa, Lord Nelson, adorned with the laurels of his magnificent victory, in fond dalliance with his frail Delilah, was basking in the courts of voluptuous and profligate kings. "No one," said Napoleon, "can surrender himself to the dominion of love, without the forfeiture of some palms of glory."

When the four vessels entered the harbor of Frejus, a signal at the mast-head of the Muiron informed the authorities on shore that Napoleon was on board. The whole town was instantly in commotion. Before the anchors were dropped the harbor was filled with boats, and the ships were surrounded with an enthusiastic multitude, climbing their sides, thronging their decks, and rending the air with their acclamations. All the laws of quarantine were disregarded. The people, weary of anarchy, and trembling in view of the approaching Austrian invasion, were almost delirious with delight in receiving thus as it were from the clouds, a deliverer, in whose potency they could implicitly trust. When warned that the ships had recently sailed from Alexandria, and that there was imminent danger that the plague, might be communicated, they replied, "We had rather have the plague than the Austrians," Breaking over all the municipal regulations of health, the people took Napoleon, almost by violence, hurried him over the side of the ship to the boats, and conveyed him in triumph to the shore. The tidings had spread from farm-house to farm-house with almost electric speed, and the whole country population, men, women, and children, were crowding down to the shore. Even the wounded soldiers in the hospital, left their cots and crawled to the beach, to get a sight of the hero. The throng became so great that it was with difficulty that Napoleon could land. The gathering multitude, however, opened to the right and the left, and Napoleon passed through them, greeted with the enthusiastic cries of "Long live the conqueror of Italy, the conqueror of Egypt, the liberator of France." The peaceful little harbor of Frejus was suddenly thrown into a state of the most unheard of excitement. The bells rang their merriest peels. The guns in the forts rolled forth their heaviest thunders over the hills and over the waves; and the enthusiastic shouts of the ever increasing multitudes, thronging Napoleon, filled the air. The ships brought the first tidings, of the wonderful victories of Mount Tabor and of Aboukir. The French, humiliated by defeat, were exceedingly elated by this restoration of the national honor. The intelligence of Napoleon's arrival was immediately communicated, by telegraph, to Paris, which was six hundred miles from Frejus.

When the tidings of Napoleon's landing of Frejus, arrived in Paris, on the evening of the 9th of October, Josephine was at a large party at the house of M. Gohier, President of the Directory. All the most distinguished men of the metropolis were there. The intelligence produced the most profound sensation. Some, rioting in the spoils of office, turned pale with apprehension; knowing well the genius of Napoleon, and his boundless popularity, they feared another revolution, which should eject them from their seats of power. Others were elated with hope; they felt that Providence had sent to France a deliverer, at the very moment when a deliverer was needed. One of the deputies, who had been deeply grieved at the disasters which were overwhelming the Republic, actually died of joy, when he heard of Napoleon's return. Josephine, intensely excited by the sudden and totally unexpected announcement, immediately withdrew, hastened home, and at midnight, without allowing an hour for repose, she entered her carriage, with Louis Bonaparte and Hortense, who subsequently became the bride of Louis, and set out to meet her husband. Napoleon almost at the same hour, with his suite, left Frejus. During every stop of his progress he was greeted with the most extraordinary demonstrations of enthusiasm and affection. Bonfires blazed from the hills, triumphed arches, hastily of maidens spread a carpet of flowers for his chariot wheels, and greeted him with smiles and choruses of welcome. He carried at Lyons in the evening. The whole city was brilliant with illuminations. An immense concourse surrounded him with almost delirious shouts of joy. The constituted authorities received him as he descended from his carriage. The major had prepared a long and eulogistic harangue for the occasion. Napoleon had no time to listen to it. With a motion of his hand, imposing silence, he said said, "Gentlemen, I learned that France was in peril, I therefore did not hesitate to leave my army in Egypt, that I might come to he rescue. I now go hence. In a few days, if you think fit to wait upon me, I shall be at leisure to hear you." Fresh horses were by this time attached to the carriages, and the cavalcade, which like a meteor had burst upon them, like a meteor disappeared. From Lyons, for some unexplained reason, Napoleon turned from the regular route to Paris and took a less frequented road. When Josephine arrived at Lyons, to her utter consternation she found that Napoleon had left the city, several hours before her arrival, and that they had passed each other by different roads. Her anguish was inexpressible. For many months she had not received a line from her idolized husband, all communication having been intercepted by the English cruisers. She knew that many, jealous her power, had disseminated, far and wide, false reports respecting her conduct. She knew that these, her enemies, would surround Napoleon immediately upon his arrival, and take advantage of her absence to inflame his mind against her. Lyons is 245 miles from Paris. Josephine had passed over those weary leagues of hill and dale, pressing on without intermission, by day and by night, alighting not for refreshment of repose. Faint, exhausted, and her heart sinking within her with fearful apprehensions of the hopeless alienation of her husband, she received the dreadful tidings that she had missed him. There was no resource left her but to retrace the steps with the utmost possible celerity. Napoleon would, however, have been one or two days in Paris before Josephine could, by any possibility, re-enter the city. Probably in all France, there was not, at that time, a more unhappy woman than Josephine.

Secret wretchedness was also gnawing at the heart of Napoleon. Who has yet fathomed the mystery of human love! Intensest love and intensest hate can, at the same moment, intertwine their fibres in inextricable blending. In nothing is the will so impotent as in guiding or checking the impulses of this omnipotent passion. Napoleon loved Josephine with that almost superhuman energy which characterized all the movements of his impetuous spirit. The stream did not fret and ripple over a shallow bed, but it was serene in its unfathomable depths. The world contained but two objects for Napoleon, glory and Josephine; glory first, and then, closely following the more substantial idol.

Many of the Parisian ladies, proud of a more exalted lineage than Josephine could boast, were exceedingly envious of the supremacy she had attained in consequence of the renown of her husband. Her influence over Napoleon was well known. Philosophers, statesmen, ambitious generals, all crowded her saloons, paying her homage. A favorable word from Josephine they knew would pave the way for them to fame and fortune. Thus Josephine, from the saloons of Paris, with milder radiance, reflected back the splendor of her husband. She solicitous of securing as many friends as possible, to aid him in future emergencies, was as diligent in "winning hearts" at home, as Napoleon was in conquering provinces abroad. The gracefulness of Josephine, her consummate delicacy of moral appreciation, her exalted intellectual gifts, the melodious tones of her winning voice, charmed courtiers, philosophers, and statesmen alike. Her saloons were ever crowded. Her entertainments were ever embellished by the presence of all who were illustrious in rank and power in the metropolis. And in whatever circles she appeared the eyes of the gentlemen first sought for her. Two resistless attractions drew them. She was peculiarly fascinating in person and in character, and, through her renowned husband, she could dispense the most precious gifts. It is not difficult to imagine the envy which must thus have been excited. Many a haughty duchess was provoked, almost beyond endurance, that Josephine, the untitled daughter of a West Indian planter, should thus engross the homage of Paris, while she, with her proud rank, her wit, and her beauty, was comparatively a cipher. Moreau's wife, in particular resented the supremacy of Josephine as a personal affront. She thought General Moreau entitled to as much consideration as General Bonaparte. By the jealousy, rankling in her own bosom, she finally succeeded in rousing her husband to conspire against Napoleon, and thus the hero of Hohenlinden was ruined. Some of the brothers and sisters of Napoleon were also jealous of the paramount influence of Josephine, and would gladly wrest a portion of it from her hands. Under these circumstances, in various ways, slander had been warily insinuated into the ears of Napoleon, respecting the conduct of his wife. Conspiring enemies became more and more bold. Josephine was represented as having forgotten her husband, as reveling exultant with female vanity, in general flirtation; and, finally, as guilty of gross infidelity. Nearly all the letters written by Napoleon and Josephine to each other, were intercepted by the English cruisers. Though Napoleon did not credit these charges in full, he cherished not a little of the pride, which led the Roman monarch to exclaim, "Caesar's wife must not be suspected."

Napoleon was in the troubled state of mind during the latter months of his residence in Egypt. One day he was sitting alone in his tent, which was pitched in the great Arabian desert. Several months had passed since he had heard a word from Josephine. Years might elapse ere they would meet again. Junot entered, having just received, through some channel of jealousy and malignity, communications from Paris. Cautiously, but fully, he unfolded the whole budget of Parisian gossip. Josephine had found, as he represented, in the love of others an ample recompense for the absence of her husband. She was surrounded by admirers with whom she was engaged in an incessant round of intrigues and flirtations. Regardless of honor she had surrendered herself to the dominion of passion. Napoleon was for a few moments in a state of terrible agitation. With hasty strides, like a chafed lion, he paced his tent, exclaiming, "Why do I love that woman so? Why can I not tear her image from my heart? I will do so. I will have an immediate and open divorce-open and public divorce." He immediately wrote to Josephine, in terms of the utmost severity accusing her of playing the coquette with half the world." The letter escaped the British cruisers and she received it. It almost broke her faithful heart. Such were the circumstances under which Napoleon and Josephine were to meet after an absence of eighteen months. Josephine was exceedingly anxious to see Napoleon before he should have an interview with her enemies. Hence the depth of anguish with which she heard her husband had passes her. Two or three days must have elapse ere she could possibly retraced the weary miles over which she had already traveled.

In the mean time the carriage of Napoleon was rapidly approaching the metropolis. By night his path was brilliant with bonfires and illuminations. The ringing of bells, the thunders of artillery, and the acclamations of the multitude, accompanied him every step of his way. But no smile of triumph played upon his pale and pensive cheeks. He felt that he was returning to a desolated home. Gloom reigned in his heart. He entered Paris, and drove rapidly to his own dwelling. Behold, Josephine was not there. Conscious guilt, he thought, had made her afraid to meet him. It is in vain to attempt to penetrate the hidden anguish of Napoleon's soul. That his proud spirit must have suffered intensity of woe no one can doubt. The bitter enemies of Josephine immediately surrounded him, eagerly taking advantage of her absence, to inflame, to a still higher degree, by adroit insinuations, his jealousy and anger. Eugene had accompanied him in his return from Egypt, and his affectionate heart ever glowed with love and admiration for his mother. With anxiety, amounting to anguish, he watched at the window for her arrival. Said one to Napoleon, maliciously endeavoring to prevent the possibility of reconciliation, "Josephine will appear before you, with all her fascinations. She will explain matters. You will forgive all, and tranquillity will be restored." "Never!" exclaimed Napoleon, with pallid cheek and trembling lip, striding nervously too and fro, through the room, "never! I forgive! ever!" Then stopping suddenly, and gazing the interlocutor wildly in the face, he exclaimed, with passionate gesticulation, "You know me. Were I not sure of my resolution, I would tear out this heart, and cast it into the fire."

How strange is the life of the heart of man. From this interview, Napoleon, two hours after his arrival in Paris with his whole soul agitated by the tumult of domestic woe, went to the palace of the Luxembourg, to visit the Directory, to form his plans for overthrow the government of France. Pale, pensive, joyless, his inflexible purposes of ambition wavered not--his iron energies yielded not. Josephine was an idol. He execrated her and he adored her. He loved her most passionately. He hated her most virulently. He could clasp her one moment to his bosom with burning kisses; the next moment he would spurn her from him with as the most loathsome wretch. But glory was a still more cherished idol, at whose shrine he bowed with unwavering adoration. He strove to forget his domestic wretchedness by prosecuting, with new vigor, his schemes of grandeur. As he ascended the stairs of the Luxembourg, some of the guard, who had been with him in Italy, recognized his person, and he was instantly greeted, with enthusiastic shouts. "Long live Bonaparte." The clamor rolled like a voice of thunder through the spacious halls of the palace, and fell, like a death knell, upon the ears of the Directors. The populace upon the pavement, caught the sound and reechoed it from street to street. The plays at the theatres, and the songs at the Opera, were stopped, that it might be announced, from the stage, that Bonaparte had arrived in Paris. Men, women, and children simultaneously rose to their feet, and a wild burst of enthusiastic joy swelled upon the night air. All Paris was in commotion. The name of Bonaparte was upon every lip. The enthusiasm was contagious. Illuminations began to blaze, here and there, without concert, from the universal rejoicing, till the whole city was resplendent with light. One bell rang forth its merry peal of greeting, and then another, and another till every steeple was vocal with its clamorous welcome. One gun was heard, rolling its heavy thunders over the city. It was the signal for an instantaneous, tumultuous roar, from artillery and musketry, from all the battalions in the metropolis. The tidings of the great victories of Aboukir and Mount Tabor, reached Paris with Napoleon. Those Oriental names were shouted through the streets, and blazed upon the eyes of the delighted people in letters of light. Thus in an hour the whole of Paris was thrown into a delirium of joy, was displayed the most triumphant and gorgeous festival.

The government of France was at the time organized somewhat upon the model of that the United States. Instead of one President, they have five, called Directors. Their Senate was called The House of Ancients; their House of Representatives, The Council of Five Hundred. The five Directors, as might have been expected, were ever quarreling among themselves, each wishing for the lion's share of power. The Monarchist, the Jacobin, and the moderate Republican could not harmoniously co-operate in the government They only circumvented each other, while the administration sank into disgrace and ruin. The Abbe'Sieyes was decidedly the most able man of the Executive. He was a proud patrician, and his character may be estimated from the following anecdote, which Napoleon has related respecting him:

"The abbe, before the revolution, was chaplain to one of the princesses. One day, when he was performing mass before herself, her attendants, and a large congregation, something occurred which rendered it necessary for the princess to leave the room. The ladies in waiting and the nobility, who attended church more out of complaisance to her than from any sense of religion followed her example. Sieyes was very busy reading his prayers, and, for a few moments, he did not perceive their departure. At last, raising his eyes from his book, behold the princess, the nobles, and all the ton had disappeared. With an air of displeasure and contempt he shut the book, and descended from the pulpit, exclaiming, 'I do not read prayers for the rabble.' He immediately went out of the chapel, leaving the service half-finished."

Napoleon arrived in Paris on the evening of the 17th of October, 1799. Two days and two nights elapse ere Josephine was able to retrace the weary leagues over which she had passed. It was the hour of midnight on the 19th when the rattle of her carriage wheels was heard entering the court-yard of their dwelling in the Rue Chanteraine. Eugene, anxiously awaiting her arrival, was instantly at his mother's side, folding her in his embrace. Napoleon also heard the arrival, but he remained sternly in his chamber. He had ever been accustomed to greet Josephine at the door of her carriage, even when she returned from an ordinary morning ride. No matter what employments engrossed his mind, no matter what guest were present, he would immediately leave every thing, and hasten to the door to assist Josephine to alight and to accompany her into the house. But now, after an absence of eighteen months, the faithful Josephine, half-dead with exhaustion, was at the door, and Napoleon, with pallid check and compressed lip, and jealousy rankling in his bosom, remained sternly in his room, preparing to overwhelm her with his indignation.

Josephine was in a state of terrible agitation. Her limbs tottered and her heart throbbed most violently. Assisted by Eugene, and accompanied by Hortense, she tremblingly ascended the stairs to the little parlor where she had so often received the caresses of her most affectionate spouse. She opened the door. There stood Napoleon, as immovable as a statue, leaning against the mantle, with his arms folded across his breast. Sternly and silently, he cast a withering look upon Josephine, and then exclaimed in tones, which, like a dagger pierced her heart "Madame! It is my wish that you retire immediately to Malmaison."

Josephine staggered and would have fallen, as if struck by a mortal blow, had she not been caught in the arms of her son. Sobbing bitterly with anguish, she was conveyed by Eugene to her own apartment. Napoleon also was dreadfully agitated. The sight of Josephine had revived all his passionate love. But he fully believed that Josephine had unpardonably trifled with his affections, that she had courted the admiration of a multitude of flatterers, and that she had degraded herself and her husband by playing the coquette. The proud spirit of Napoleon could not brook such a requital for his fervid love. With hasty strides he traversed the room, striving to nourish his indignation. The sobs of Josephine had deeply moved him. He yearned to fold her again in fond love to his heart. But he proudly resolved that he would not relent. Josephine, with that prompt obedience which ever characterized her, prepared immediately to comply with his orders. It was midnight. For a week she had lived in her carriage almost without food or sleep. Malmaison was thirty miles from Paris. Napoleon did not suppose that she would leave the house until morning. Much to his surprise, in a few moments he heard Josephine, Eugene, and Hortense descending the stairs to take the carriage. Napoleon, even in his anger, could not be thus inhuman. "My heart," he said, "was never formed to witness tears without emotion." He immediately descended to the court-yard, though his pride would not yet allow him to speak to Josephine. He, however, addressing Eugene, urged the party to return and obtain refreshment and repose. Josephine, all submission, unhesitatingly yielded to his wishes, and re-ascending the stairs, in the extremity of exhaustion and grief, threw herself upon a couch, in her apartment. Napoleon, equally wretched, returned to his cabinet. Two days of utter misery passed away, during which no intercourse took place between the estranged parties, each of whom loved the other with almost superhuman intensity.

Love in the heart will finally triumph over all obstructions. The struggle was long, but gradually pride and passion yielded, and love regained the ascendency. Napoleon so far surrendered on the third day, as to enter the apartment of Josephine. She was seated at a toilet-table, her face buried in her hands, and absorbed in the profoundest woe. The letters, which she had received from Napoleon, and which she had evidently been reading, were spread upon the table. Hortense the picture of grief and despair, was standing in the alcove of a window. Napoleon had opened the door softly, and his entrance had not been heard. With an irresolute step he advanced toward his wife, and then said, kindly and sadly, "Josephine!" She started at the sound of that well-known voice, and raising her swollen eyes, swimming in tears, mournfully exclaimed, "Monami" --my friend . This was the term of endearment with which she had invariably addressed her husband. It recalled a thousand delightful reminiscences. Napoleon was vanquished. He extended his hand. Josephine threw herself into his arms, pillowed her aching head upon his bosom, and in the intensity of blended joy and anguish, wept convulsively. A long explanation ensued. Napoleon became satisfied that Josephine had been deeply wronged. The reconciliation was cordial and entire, and was never again interrupted.

Napoleon now, with a stronger heart, turned to the accomplishment of his designs to rescue France from anarchy. He was fully conscious of his own ability to govern the nation. He knew that it was the almost unanimous wish of the people that he should grasp the reins of power. He was confident of their cordial co-operation in any plans he might adopt. Still it was an enterprise of no small difficulty to thrust the five Directors from their thrones, and to get the control of the Council of Ancients and of The Five Hundred. Never was a difficult achievement more adroitly and proudly accomplished.

For many days Napoleon almost entirely secluded himself from observation, affecting a studious avoidance of the public gaze. He laid aside his military dress and assumed the peaceful costume of the National Institute. Occasionally he wore a beautiful Turkish sabre, suspended by a silk ribbon. This simple dress transported the imagination of the beholder to Aboukir, Mount Tabor, and the Pyramids. He studiously sought the society of literary men, and devoted to them his attention. He invited distinguished men of the Institute to dine with him, and avoiding political discussion, conversed only upon literary and scientific subjects.

Moreau and Bernadotte were the two rival generals from whom Napoleon had the most to fear. Two days after his arrival in Paris Napoleon said to Bourrienne, "I believe that I shall have Bernadotte and Moreau against me. But I do not fear Moreau. He is devoid of energy. He prefers military to political power. We shall gain him by the promise of a command. But Bernadotte has Moorish blood in his veins. He is bold and enterprising. He does not like me, and I am certain that he will oppose me. If he should become ambitious he will venture anything. Besides, this fellow is not to be seduced. He is disinterested and clever. But, after all, we have just arrived. We shall see."

Napoleon formed no conspiracy. He confided to no one his designs. And yet, in his own solitary mind, relying entirely upon his own capacious resources, he studied the state of affairs and he matured his plans. Sieyes was the only one whose talents and influence Napoleon feared. The abbe also looked with apprehension upon his formidable rival. They stood aloof and eyed each other. Meeting at a dinner party, each was too proud to make advances. Yet each thought only of the other. Mutually exasperated, they separated without having spoken. "Did you see that insolent little fellow?" said Sieyes, "he would not even condescend to notice a member of the government, who, if they had done right, would have caused him to be shot." "What on earth," said Napoleon, "could have induced them to put that priest in the Directory. He is sold to Prussia. Unless you take care, he will deliver you up to that power." Napoleon dined with Moreau, who afterward in hostility to Napoleon pointed the guns of Russia against the columns of his countrymen. The dinner party was at (Gohier's, one of the Directors. The following interesting conversation took place between the rival generals. When first introduced, they looked at each other a moment without speaking, Napoleon, conscious of his own superiority, and solicitous to gain the powerful co-operation of Moreau, made the first advances, and, with great courtesy, expressed the earnest desire he felt to make his acquaintance. "You have returned victorious from Egypt." replied Moreau, "and I from Italy after a great defeat. It was the month which General Joubert passed in Pairs after his marriage, which caused our disasters. This gave the allies time to reduce Mantua, and to bring up the force which besieged it to take a part in the action. It is always the greater number which defeats the less." "True," replied Napoleon, "it is always, the greater number which beats the less" "And yet," said Gohier, "with small armies you have frequently defeated large ones." "Even then," rejoined Napoleon, "it was always the inferior force which was defeated by the superior. When with a small body of men I was in the presence of a large one, collecting my little band, I fell like lightning on one of the wings of the hostile army, and defeated it. Profiting by the disorder which such an event never failed to occasion in their whole line, I repeated the attack, with similar success, in another quarter, still with my whole force. I thus beat it in detail. The general victory which was the result, was still an example of the truth of the principle that the greater force defeats the lesser." Napoleon, by those fascinations of mind and manner, which enabled him to win to him whom he would, soon gained an ascendency over Moreau. And when, two days after, in token of his regard, he sent him a beautiful poniard set with diamonds, worth two thousand dollars: the work was accomplished, and Moreau was ready to do his bidding. Napoleon gave a small and very select dinner party. Gohier was invited. The conversation turned on the turquoise used by the Orientals to clasp their turbans. Napoleon, rising from the table took from a private drawer, two very beautiful brooches, richly set with those jewels. One he gave to Gohier, the other to his tried friend Desaix. "It is a little toy," said he, "which we republicans may give and receive without impropriety." The Director, flattered by the delicacy of the compliment, and yet not repelled by any thing assuming the grossness of a bribe, yielded his heart's homage to Napoleon.

Republican France was surrounded by monarchies in arms against her. Their hostility was so inveterate, and, from the very nature of the case, so inevitable, that Napoleon thought that France should ever be prepared for an attack, and that the military spirit should be carefully fostered. Republican America, most happily, has no foe to fear, and all her energies may be devoted to filling the land with peace and plenty, But a republic in monarchical Europe must sleep by the side of its guns. "Do you, really," said Napoleon, to Gohier, in this interview, "advocate a general peace! You are wrong. The Republic should never make but partial accommodations. It should always contrive to have some war on hand to keep alive the military spirit." We can, perhaps, find a little extenuation for this remark, in its apparent necessity, and in the influences of the martial ardor in which Napoleon from his very infancy had been enveloped. Even now, it is to be feared that the time is far distant ere the nations of the earth can learn war no more.

Lefebvre was commandant of the guard of the two legislative bodies. His co-operation was important. Napoleon sent a special invitation for an interview. "Lefebvre," said he, "will you, one of the pillars of the Republic, suffer it to perish in the hands of these lawyers ? Join me and assist to save it." Taking from his own side the beautiful Turkish scimitar which he wore, he passed the ribbon over Lefebvre's neck, saying, "accept this sword, which I wore at the battle of the Pyramids. I give it to you as a token of my esteem and confidence." "Yes," replied Lefebvre, most highly gratified at this signal mark of confidence and generosity, "let us throw the lawyers into the river."

Napoleon soon had an interview with Bernadotte. "He confessed," said Napoleon to Bourrienne, "that he thought us all lost. He spoke of external enemies, of internal enemies, and, at that word he looked steadily in my face. I also gave him a glance. But patience; the pear will soon be ripe."

In this interview Napoleon inveighed against the violence and lawlessness of the Jacobin club. "Your own brothers," Bernadotte replied, "were the founders of that club. And yet you reproach me with favoring its principles. It is to the instructions of some one, I know not who , that we are to ascribe the agitation which now prevails." "True, general," Napoleon replied, most vehemently, "and I would rather live in the woods, than in a society which presents no security against violence." This conversation only strengthened the alienation already existing between them.

Bernadotte, though a brave and efficient officer, was a jealous braggadocio. At the first interview between these two distinguished men, when Napoleon was in command of the army of Italy, they contemplated each other with mutual dislike. "I have seen a man," said Bernadotte, "of twenty-six or seven years of age, who assumes the air of one of fifty; and he presages any thing but good to the Republic." Napoleon summarily dismissed Bernadotte by saying, "he has a French head and a Roman heart."

There were three political parties now dividing France, the old royalist party, in favor of the restoration of the Bourbons; the radical democrats, or Jacobins, with Barras at its head, supported by the mob of Paris; and the moderate republicans led by Sieyes. All these parties struggling together, and fearing each other, in the midst of the general anarchy which prevailed, immediately paid court to Napoleon, hoping to secure the support of his all-powerful arm.

Napoleon determined to co-operate with the moderate republicans. The restoration of the Bourbons was not only out of the question, but Napoleon had no more power to secure that result, than had Washington to bring the United States into peaceful submission to George III. "Had I joined the Jacobins," said Napoleon, "I should have risked nothing. But after conquering with them, it would have been necessary almost immediately, to conquer against them. A club can not endure a permanent chief. It wants one for every successive passion. Now to make use of a party one day, in order to attack it the next, under whatever pretext it is done, is still an act of treachery. It was inconsistent with my principles."

Sieyes, the head of the moderate republicans, and Napoleon soon understood each other, and each admitted the necessity of co-operation. The government was in a state of chaos. "Our salvation now demands," said the wily diplomatist, "both a head and a sword." Napoleon had both. In one fortnight from the time when he landed at Frejus, "the pear was ripe." The plan was all matured for the great conflict. Napoleon, in solitary grandeur, kept his own counsel. He had secured the cordial co-operation, the unquestioning obedience of all his subordinates. Like the general upon the field of battle, he was simply to give his orders, and columns marched, and squadrons charged, and generals swept the field in unquestioning obedience. Though he had determined to ride over and to destroy the existing government, he wished to avail himself, so far as possible, of the mysterious power of law, as a conqueror turns a captured battery upon the foe from whom it had been wrested. Such a plot, so simple, yet so bold and efficient, was never formed before. And no one, but another Napoleon, will be able to execute another such again. All Paris was in a state of intense excitement. Something great was to be done. Napoleon was to do it. But nobody knew when, or what, or how. All impatiently awaited orders. The majority of the Senate, or Council of Ancients, conservative in its tendencies, and having once seen, during the reign of terror, the horrors of Jacobin domination, were ready, most obsequiously, to rally beneath the banner of so resolute a leader as Napoleon. They were prepared, without question, to pass any vote which he should propose. The House of Representatives or Council of Five Hundred, more democratic in its constitution, contained a large number of vulgar, ignorant, and passionate demagogues, struggling to grasp the reins of power. Carnot, whose co-operation Napoleon had entirely secured, was President of the Senate. Lucien Bonaparte, the brother of Napoleon, was Speaker of the House. The two bodies met in the palace of the Tuileries. The constitution conferred upon the Council of Ancients, the right to decide upon the place of meeting for both legislative assemblies.

All the officers of the garrison in Paris, and all the distinguished military men in the metropolis, had solicited the honor of a presentation to Napoleon. Without any public announcement, each one was privately informed that Napoleon would see him on the morning of the 9th of November. All the regiments in the city had also solicited the honor of a review by the distinguished conqueror. They were also informed that Napoleon would review them early on the morning of the 9th of November. The Council of Ancients was called to convene at six o'clock on the morning of the same day. The Council of Five Hundred were also to convene at 11 o'clock of the same morning. This, the famous 18th of Brumaire, was the destined day for the commencement of the great struggle. These appointments were given in such a way as to attract no public attention. The general-in-chief was thus silently arranging his forces for the important conflict. To none did he reveal those combinations, by which he anticipated a bloodless victory.

The morning of the 9th of November arrived. The sun rose with unwonted splendor over the domes of the thronged city. A more brilliant day never dawned. Through all the streets of the mammoth metropolis there was heard, in the earliest twilight of the day, the music of martial bands, the tramp of battalions, the clatter of iron hoofs, and the rumbling of heavy artillery wheels over the pavements, as regiments of infantry, artillery, and cavlary, in the proudest array, marched to the Boulevards to receive the honor of a review from the conqueror of Italy and of Egypt. The whole city was in commotion, guided by the unseen energies of Napoleon in the retirement of his closet. At eight o'clock Napoleon's house, in the Rue Chanteraine, was so thronged with illustrious military men, in most brilliant uniform, that every room was filled and even the street was crowded with the resplendent guests. At that moment the Council of Ancients passed the decree, which Napoleon had prepared, that the two legislative bodies should transfer their meeting to St. Cloud, a few miles from Paris; and that Napoleon Bonaparte should be put in command of all the military forces in the city, to secure the public peace. The removal to St. Cloud was a merciful precaution against bloodshed. It secured the legislatures from the ferocious interference of a Parisian mob. The President of the Council was himself commissioned to bear the decree to Napoleon. He elbowed his way through the brilliant throng, crowding the door and the apartment of Napoleon's dwelling, and presented to him the ordinance. Napoleon was ready to receive it. He stepped upon the balcony, gathered his vast retinue of powerful guests before him, and in a loud and firm voice, read to them the decree. "Gentlemen," said he, "will you help me save the Republic?" One simultaneous burst of enthusiasm rose from every lip, as drawing their swords from their scabbards they waved them in the air and shouted, "We swear it, we swear it." The victory was virtually won. Napoleon was now at the head of the French nation. Nothing remained but to finish his conquest. There was no retreat left open for his foes. There was hardly the possibility of a rally. And now Napoleon summoned all his energies to make his triumph most illustrious. Messengers were immediately sent to read the decree to the troops already assembled, in the utmost display of martial pomp, to greet the idol of the army, and who were in a state of mind to welcome him most exultingly as their chief. A burst of enthusiastic acclamation ascended from their ranks which almost rent the skies. Napoleon immediately mounted his horse, and, surrounded by the most magnificent staff, whom he had thus ingeniously assembled at his house, and, accompanied by a body of fifteen hundred cavalry, whom he had taken the precaution to rendezvous near his dwelling proceeded to the palace of the Tuileries. The gorgeous spectacle burst like a vision upon astonished Paris. It was Napoleon's first public appearance. Dressed in the utmost simplicity of a civilian's costume, he rode upon his magnificent charger, the centre of all eyes. The gleaming banners, waving in the breeze, and the gorgeous trappings of silver and gold, with which his retinue was embellished, set off in stronger relief the majestic simplicity of his own appearance. With the pump and the authority of an enthroned king, Napoleon entered the Council of the Ancients. The Ancients themselves were dazzled by his sudden apparition in such imposing and unexpected splendor and power. Ascending the bar, attended by an imposing escort, he addressed the assembly and took his oath of office. "You," said Napoleon, "are the wisdom of the nation. To you it belongs to concert measures for the salvation of the Republic. I come, surrounded by our generals, to offer you support. Faithfully will I fulfill the task you have intrusted to me. Let us not look into the pass for precedents. nothing in history resembles the eighteenth century. Nothing in the eighteenth century resembles the present moment."

An aid was immediately sent to the palace of the Luxembourg, to inform the five Directors, there in session, of the decree. Two of the Directors, Sieyes and Ducos, were pledged to Napoleon, and immediately resigned their offices, and hastened to the Tuileries. Barras, bewildered and indignant, sent his secretary with a remonstrance. Napoleon, already assuming the authority of an emperor, and speaking as if France were his patrimony, came down upon him with a torrent of invective. "Where." he indignantly exclaimed, "is that beautiful France which I left you so brilliant! I left you peace. I find war. I left you victories. I find but defeats. I left you millions of Italy. I find taxation and beggary. Where are the hundred thousand men, my companions in glory! They are dead. This state of things can not continue. It will lead to despotism." Barras was terrified. He feared to have Napoleon's eagle eye investigate his peculations. He resigned. Two Directors only now were left, Gohier and Moulins. It took a majority of the five to constitute a quorum. The two were powerless. In despair of successful resistance and fearing vengeance they hastened to the Tuileries to find Napoleon. They were introduced to him surrounded by Sieyes, Ducos, and a brilliant staff. Napoleon received them cordially. "I am glad to see you," said he. "I doubt not that you will both sign. Your patriotism will not allow you to appose a revolution which is both inevitable and necessary." "I do not yet despair," said Gohier, vehemently, "aided by my colleage, Moulins, of saving the Republic." "With what will you save it?" exclaimed Napoleon. "With the Constitution which is crumbling to pieces?" Just at that moment a messenger came in and informed the Directors that Santeree, the brewer, who, during the Reign of Terror, had obtained a bloody celebrity as leader of the Jacobins, was rousing the mob in the faubourgs to resistance. "General Moulins," said Napoleon, firmly, "you are the friend of Santerre. Tell him that at the very first movement he makes, I will cause him to be shot." Moulins, exasperated yet appalled, made an apologetic reply. "The Republic is in danger," said Napoleon. We must save it. It is my will . Sieyes, Ducos, and Barras have resigned. You are two individuals insulated and powerless. I advise you not to resist." They still refused. Napoleon had no time to spend in parleying. He immediately sent them both back into the Luxembourg, separated them and placed them under arrest. Fouche, * occupying the important post of Minister of Police, though not in Napoleon's confidence, yet anxious to display his homage to the rising luminary, called upon Napoleon and informed him that he had closed the barriers, and had thus prevented all ingress or egress. "What means this folly?" said Napoleon. "Let those orders be instantly countermanded. Do we not march with the opinion of the nation, and by its strength alone? Let no citizen be interrupted. Let every publicity be given to what is done."

"Fouche," said Napoleon, is a miscreant of all colors, a terrorist, and one who took an active part in many bloody scenes of the Revolution. He is a man who can worm all your secrets out of you, with an air of calmness and unconcern. He is very rich; but his riches have been badly acquired. He never was my confidant. Never did he approach me without bending to the ground. But I never had any esteem for him. I employed him merely as an instrument."

The Council of Five Hundred, in great confusion and bewilderment, assembled at eleven o'clock. Lucien immediately communicated the degree transferring their session to St. Cloud. This cut off all debate. The decree was perfectly legal. There could therefore be no legal pretext for opposition. Napoleon, the idol of the army, had the whole military power obedient to his nod. Therefore resistance of any kind was worse than folly. The deed was adroitly done. At eleven o'clock the day's work was accomplished. There was no longer a Directory. Napoleon was the appointed chief of the troops, and they were filling the streets with enthusiastic shouts of "Live Napoleon." The Council of Ancients were entirely at his disposal. An a large party in the Council of Five Hundred were also wholly subservient to his will. Napoleon, proud, silent, reserved reserved, fully conscious of his own intellectual supremacy, and regarding the generals, the statesmen, and the multitude around him, as a man contemplates children, ascended the grand staircase of the Tuileries as it were his hereditary home. Nearly all parties united to sustain his triumph. Napoleon was a solider. The guns of Paris joyfully thundered forth the victory of one who seemed the peculiar favorite of the God of war. Napoleon was a scholar, stimulating intellect to its mightiest achievements. The scholars of Paris, gratefully united to weave a chaplet for the brow of their honored associate and patron. Napoleon was, for those days of profligacy and unbridled lust, a model of purity of morals, and of irreproachable integrity. The proffered bribe of millions could not tempt him. The dancing daughters of Herodias, with all their blandishments, could not lure him from his life of Herculean toil and from his majestic patriotism. The wine which glitters in the cup, never vanquished him. At the shrine of no vice was he found a worshiper. The purest and the best in France, disgusted with that gilded corruption which had converted the palaces of the Bourbons into harems of voluptuous sin, and still more deeply loathing that vulgar and revolting vice, which had transformed Paris into a house of infamy, enlisted all their sympathies in behalf of the exemplary husband and the incorruptible patriot. Napoleon was one of the most firm and unflinching friends of law and order. France was weary of anarchy and was trembling under the apprehension that the gutters of the guillotine were again to be clotted with blood. And mothers and maidens prayed for God's blessing upon Napoleon, who appeared to them as a messenger sent from Heaven for their protection.

During the afternoon and the night his room at the Tuileries was thronged with the most illustrious statesmen, generals, and scholars of Paris, hastening to pledge to him their support. Napoleon, perfectly unembarrassed and never at a loss in any emergency, gave his orders for the ensuing day. Lannes was intrusted with a body of troops to guard the Tuileries. Murat, who, said Napoleon, "was superb at Aboukir," with a numerous cavalry and a crops of grenadiers was stationed at St. Cloud, a thunderbolt in Napoleon's right hand. Woe betide the mob into whose ranks that thunderbolt may be hurled. Moreau, with five hundred men, was stationed to guard the Luxembourg, where the two refractory Directors were held under arrest. Serrurier was posted in a commanding position with a strong reserve, prompt for any unexpected exigence. Even a body of troops were sent to accompany Barras to his country seat, ostensibly as an escort of honor, but in reality to guard against any change in that venal and versatile mind. The most energetic measures were immediately adopted to prevent any rallying point for the disaffected. Bills were everywhere posted, exhorting the citizens to be quiet, and assuring them that powerful efforts were making to save the Republic. These minute precaution were characteristic of Napoleon. He believed in destiny. Yet he left nothing for destiny to accomplish. He ever sought to make provision for all conceivable contingencies. These measures were completely successful. Though Paris was in a delirium of excitement, there were outbreaks of lawless violence. Neither Monarchist, Republican, nor Jacobin knew what Napoleon intended to do. All were conscious that he would do something. It was known that the Jacobin party in the Council of Five Hundred on the ensuing day, would make a desperate effort at resistance. Sieyes, perfectly acquainted with revolutionary movements, urged Napoleon to arrest some forty of the Jacobins most prominent in the Council. This would have secured an easy victory on the morrow. Napoleon, however, rejected the advice, saying, "I pledged my word this morning to protect the national representation. I will not this evening violate my oath." Had the Assembly been convened in Paris, all the mob of the faubourgs would have risen, like an inundation, in their behalf, and torrents of blood must have been shed. The sagacious transferrence of the meeting to St. Cloud, several miles from Paris, saved those lives. The powerful military display, checked any attempt at a march upon St. Cloud. What could the mob do, with Murat, Lannes, and Serrurier, guided by the energies of Napoleon, ready to hurl their solid columns upon them!

The delicacy of attention with which Napoleon treated Josephine, was one of the most remarkable traits in his character. It is not strange that he should have won from her a love almost more than human. During the exciting scenes of this day, when no one could tell whether events were guiding him to a crown or to the guillotine, Napoleon did not forget his wife, who was awaiting the result, with deep solicitude, in her chamber in the Rue Chanteraine. Nearly every hour he dispatched a messenger to Josephine, with a hastily written line communicating to her the progress of events. Late at night he returned to his home, apparently has fresh and unexhausted as in the morning. He informed Josephine minutely of the scenes of the day, and then threw himself upon a sofa, for an hour's repose. Early the next morning he was on horseback, accompanied by a regal retinue, directing his steps to St. Cloud. Three halls had been prepared in the palace; one for the Ancients, one for the Five Hundred, and one for Napoleon. He thus assumed the position which he knew it to be the almost unanimous will of the nation that he should fill. During the night the Jacobins had arranged a very formidable resistance. Napoleon was considered to be in imminent peril. He would be denounced as a traitor. Sieyes and Ducos had each a post-chaise and six horses, waiting at the gate of St. Cloud, prepared, in case of reverse, to escape for life. There were many ambitious generals, ready to mount the crest of any refluent wave to sweep Napoleon to destruction. Benadotte was the most to be feared. Orders were given to cut down the first person who should attempt to harangue the troops. Napoleon, riding at the head of this imposing military display, manifested no agitation. He knew, however, perfectly well the capriciousness of the popular voice, and that the multitude in the same hour could cry "Hosanna!" and "crucify!" The two Councils met. The tumult in the Five Hundred was fearful. Cries of "Down with the dictator!" "Death to the tyrant!" "Live the Constitution!" filled the hall, and drowned the voice of deliberation. The friends of Napoleon were swept before the flood of passion. It was proposed that every member should immediately take anew the oath to support the Constitution. No one dared to peril his life by the refusal. Even Lucien, the Speaker, was compelled to descend from his chair and take the oath. The Ancients, overawed by the unexpected violence of this opposition in the lower and more popular house, began to be alarmed and to recede. The opposition took a bold and aggressive stand, and proposed a decree of outlawry against Napoleon. The friends of Napoleon, remembering past scenes of earnage, were timid and yielding. Defeat seemed inevitable. Victory was apparently turned into discomfiture and death. In this emergency Napoleon displayed the same coolness, energy, and tact with which so often, on the field of battle, in the most disastrous hour, he had rolled back the tide of defeat in the resplendent waves of victory. His own mind was the corps de reserve which he now marched into the conflict to arrest the rout of his friends. Taking with him a few aids and a band of grenadiers, he advanced to the door of the hall. On his way he met Bernadotte. "You are marching to the guillotine, " said his rival, sternly. "We shall see," Napoleon coolly replied. Leaving the soldiers, with their glittering steel and nodding plumes, at the entrance of the room, he ascended the tribune. The hush of perfect silence pervaded the agitated hall. "Gentlemen," said he, "you are on a volcano. You deemed the Republic in danger. You called me to your aid. I obeyed. And now I am assailed by a thousand calumnies. They talk of Caesar, of Cromwell, of military despotism, as if any thing in antiquity resembled the present moment.

Danger presses. Disaster thickens. We have no longer a government. The Directors have resigned. The Five Hundred are in a tumult. Emissaries are instigating Paris to revolt. Agitators would gladly bring back the revolutionary tribunals. But fear not. Aided by my companions in arms I will protect you. I desire nothing for myself, but to save the Republic. And I solemnly swear to protect that liberty and equality , for which we have made such sacrifices." "And the Constitution !" some one cried out. Napoleon had purposely omitted the Constitution in his oath, for he despised it, and was at that moment laboring for its overthrow. He paused for a moment, and then, with increasing energy exclaimed, "The institution! you have none. You violated when the Executive infringed the rights of the Legislature. You violated it when the Legislature struck at the independence of the Executive. You violated it when, with sacriligious hand, both the Legislature and Executive struck at the sovereignty of the people, by annulling their elections. The Constitution! It is a mockery; invoked by all, regarded by none."

Rallied by the presence of Napoleon, and by these daring words, his friends recovered their courage, and two-thirds of the Assembly rose in expression of their confidence and support. At this moment intelligence arrived that the Five Hundred were compelling Lucien to put to the vote Napoleon's outlawry. Not an instant was to be lost. There is a mysterious power in law. The passage of that vote would probably have been fatal. Life and death were trembling in the balance. "I would then have given two hundred millions," said Napoleon, "to have had Ney by my side." Turning to the Ancients, he exclaimed, "if any orator, paid by foreigners, shall talk of outlawing me, I will appeal for protection to my brave companions in arms, whose plumes are nodding at the door. Remember that I march accompanied by the God of fortune and by the God of war."

He immediately left the Ancients, and, attended by his military band, hastened to the Council of Five Hundred. On his way he met Augereau, who was pale and trembling, deeming Napoleon lost. "You have got yourself into a pretty fix," said he, with deep agitation. "Matters were worse at Arcola," Napoleon coolly replied. "Keep quiet. All will be changed in half an hour." Followed by his grenadiers, he immediately entered the Hall of the Five Hundred. The soldiers remained near the door. Napoleon traversed alone half of the room to reach the bar. It was an hour in which nothing could save him but the resources of his own mind. Furious shouts rose from all parts of the house. "What means this! down with the tyrant! begone!" "The winds," says Napoleon, "suddenly escaping from the caverns of Aeolus can give but a faint idea of that tempest." In the midst of the horrible confusion he in vain endeavored to speak. The members, in the wildest fray, crowded around him. The grenadiers witnessing the peril of their chief rushed to his rescue. A dagger was struck at his bosom. A soldier, with his arm, parried the blow. With their bayonets they drove back the members, and encircling Napoleon, bore him from the Hall. Napoleon had hardly descended the outer steps ere some one informed him that his brother Lucien was surrounded by the infuriated deputies, and that his life was in imminent jeopardy. "Colonel Dumoulin," said he, "take a battalion of grenadiers and hasten to my brother's deliverance." The soldiers rushed into the room, drove back the crowd who, with violent menaces, were surrounding Lucien, and saying, "It is by your brother's commands," escorted him in safety out of the ball into the court-yard. Napoleon, now mounting his horse, with Lucien by his side, rode along in front of his troops." The Council of Five Hundred," exclaimed Lucien, "is dissolved. It is I that tell you so. Assassins have taken possession of the hall of meeting. I summon you to march and clear it of them." "Soldiers!" said

Napoleon, "can I rely upon you!" .... "Long live Bonaparte," was the simultaneous response Murat took a battalion of grenadiers and marched to the entrance of the hall. When Murat headed a column it was well known that there would be no child's play. "Charge bayonets, forward!" he exclaimed, with imperturbable coolness. The drums beat the charge. Steadily the bristling line of steel advanced. The terrified representatives leaped over the benches, rushed through the passage ways, and sprang out of the windows, throwing upon the floor, in their precipitate flight, gowns, scarfs, and hats. In two minutes the hall was cleared. As the Representatives were flying in dismay across the garden, on officer proposed that the soldiers should be ordered to fire upon them. Napoleon decisively refused, saying, "It is my wish that not a single drop of blood be split."

As Napoleon wished to avail himself as far as possible, of the forms of law, he assembled the two legislative bodies in the evening. Those only attended who were friendly to his cause. Unanimously they decreed that Napoleon had deserved well of his country; they abolished the Directory. The executive power they vested in Napoleon, Sieyes, and Ducos, with the title of Consuls. Two committees of twenty-five members each, taken from the two Councils, were appointed to co-operate with the Consuls in forming a new Constitution. During the evening the rumor reached Paris that Napoleon had failed in his enterprise. The consternation was great. The mass of the people, of all ranks, dreading the renewal of revolutionary horrors, and worn out with past convulsions, passionately longed for repose Their only hope was in Napoleon. At nine o'clock at night intelligence of the change of government was officially announced, by a proclamation which the victor had dictated with the rapidity and the glowing eloquence which characterized all of his mental acts. It was read by torchlight to assembled and deeply agitated groups, all over the city. The welcome tidings were greeted with the liveliest demonstrations of applause. At three o'clock in the morning Napoleon threw himself into his carriage to return to Paris. Bourrienne accompanied him. Napoleon appeared so absorbed in thought, that he uttered not one single word during the ride.

At four o'clock in the morning he alighted from his carriage, at the door of his dwelling in the Rue Chanteraine. Josephine, in the greatest anxiety, was watching at the window for his approach. Napoleon had not been able to send her one single line during the turmoil and the peril of that eventful day. She sprang to meet him. Napoleon foundly encircled her in his arms, briefly recapitulated the scenes of the day, and assured her that since he had taken the oath of office, he had not allowed himself to speak to a single individual, for he wished that the beloved voice of his Josephine might be the first to congratulate him upon his virtual accession to the Empire of France. The heart of Josephine could appreciate a delicacy of love so refined and so touching. Well might she say, "Napoleon is the most fascinating of men." It was then after four o'clock in the morning. The dawn of the day to conduct Napoleon to a new scene of Herculean toil in organizing the Republic Throwing himself upon a couch, for a few moments of repose, he exclaimed, gayly, "good-night, my Josephine! To-morrow, we sleep in the palace of the Luxembourg."

Napoleon was then but twenty-nine years of age. And yet, under circumstances of inconceivable difficulty, with unhesitating reliance upon his own mental resources, he assumed the enormous care of creating and administering a Lew government for thirty millions of people. Never did he achieve a victory which displayed more consummate genius. On no occasion of his life did his majestic intellectual power beam forth with more brilliance. It is not to be expected that, for ages to come, the world will be united in opinion respecting this transaction. Some represent it as an outrage against law and liberty. Others consider it a necessary act which put an end to corruption and anarchy. That the course which Napoleon pursued was in accordance with the wished of the overwhelming majority of the French people on one can doubt. It is questionable whether, even now, France is prepared for self-government. There can be no question that then the republic had totally failed. Said Napoleon, in reference to this revolution, "For my part, all my share of the plot, was confined to assembling the crowd of my visitors at the same hour in the morning, and marching at their head to seize upon power. It was from the threshold of my door, and without my friends having any previous knowledge of my intentions, that I led them to this conquest. p It was amidst the brilliant escort which they formed, their lively joy and unanimous ardor, that I presented myself a the bar of the Ancients to thank them for the dictatorship with which they invested me. Metaphysicians have disputed and will long dispute, whether we did not violate the laws, and whether we were not criminal. But these are mere abstractions which should disappear before imperious necessity. One might as well blame a sailor for waste and destruction, when he cuts away a mast to save his ship. the fact is, had it not been for us the country must have been lost. We saved it. The authors of that memorable state transaction ought to answer their accusers proudly, like the Roman, 'We protest that we have saved our country. Come with us and render thanks to the Gods.'"

With the exception of the Jacobins all parties were strongly in favor of this revolution. For ten years the people had been so accustomed to the violation of the laws, that they had ceased to condemn such acts, and judged of them only by their consequences. All over France the feeling was nearly universal in favor of the new government. Says Alison, who surely will not be accused of regarding Napoleon with a partial eye, "Napoleon rivaled Caesar in the elemency with which he used his victory. No proscriptions or massacres, few arrests or imprisonments followed the triumph of order over revolution. On the contrary, numerous acts of merey, as wise as they were magnanimous, illustrated the rise of the consular throne. The elevation of Napoleon was not only unstained by blood, but not even a single captive long lamented the car of the victor. A signal triumph of the principles of humility over those of cruelty, glorious alike to the actors and the age in which it occurred: and a memorable proof how much more durable are the victories obtained by moderation and wisdom, than those achieved by violence and stained by blood." ˜

###

13464684R00072

Printed in Great Britain
by Amazon.co.uk, Ltd.,
Marston Gate.